Who
Did You See?

A Journey of Forgiveness, Healing and Restoration

Pamela Chastain

Copyright © 2019 Pamela Chastain

All rights reserved. Except as permitted under the U.S. Copyright Act of 1976, no part of this publication may be reproduced, distributed, or transmitted in any form or by any means, or stored in a database or retrieval system, without the prior written permission of the publisher.

One11 Publishing
Lindenhurst, IL 60048

www.one11publishing.com

Publisher: Sedrik Newbern, Newbern Consulting, LLC
Editor: Linda Wolf, Network Typesetting, Inc.
Cover Designer: Joshua Swodeck, Swodeck, Inc.

Printed in the United States of America
First Edition: April 2019

Author's Note
The stories in this book reflect the author's recollection of events. Some names, locations, and identifying characteristics have been changed to protect the privacy of those depicted. Dialogue has been re-created from memory.

ISBN Paperback 978-1-7329512-2-8
ISBN Digital 978-1-7329512-3-5

Library of Congress Control Number: 2019903151

One11 Publishing is an imprint of
Newbern Consulting, LLC.

Dedication

This book is dedicated to all the people who choose to love me, flaws and all.

To my husband, Alan, who never ceases to amaze me with the depth of his love. Thank you for always being on my side.

To Alec, who I hope learns to give as much grace as he is given. I have never given up on him, will never give up on him, and will always love him unconditionally.

To my beautiful Krista Grace, who has no idea the depth of her strength. She has more integrity, beauty, and enduring love than anyone I have ever known. I cannot wait to see where this life will take her.

To Jack, who amazes me more every single day. His quiet demeanor and steadfast love will be a gift to everyone who will ever have the pleasure of being included in his circle.

To Evan, having your join my brood and watching you finish high school has brought me immeasurable joy. I love you, and I am so proud of the man you are becoming.

To the many friends who have picked me up, cried with me, laughed with me, and loved me so much more than I was capable of giving back—thank you.

Last but not least, this book is dedicated to everyone who has endured the pain of sexual abuse. Don't let it define you; let it become just a piece in your complex puzzle as you create your beautiful new life.

Contents

Dedication i
Acknowledgements i
Introduction iii
Finally Finding Bliss 1
Alan Chastain 2
Stewie 6
My Life Rope 14
Krista Grace 22
My Warrior 29
Becoming A Real Father 32
Little Jack 38
Shame 43
Power 48
Anger 53
Sense of Loss 57
Momma – The Early Years 60
The Tables Will Turn 66
The Cycle of Abuse 74
Along Came Prince Charming - The First One 79
Coming Home 89
Coming Home – Scene 2 97
Facing The Past 104

Two Decades in Prison 112
Hunter 122
FREEDOM 125
Husband Number 3 132
Starting Over – Again.. 144
Are We Different? 152
Things Always Get Worse Before They Get Better. 159
We Find Ourselves Back At the Beginning 164
About the Author 169

Acknowledgements

    I have so many people to publicly thank for their help with completing this labor of love. First and foremost, thank you to my publisher Sedrik Newbern for believing in me. Thank you for coaching, listening and advising me for the last several years. Even when I didn't know if I could tell my story, you believed in me.

    Thank you to Angel Noble and Laquita Scaife for walking this road with me! When I thought the book was done, they read it and helped me to see things from the reader's perspective. I couldn't have done this without you two beautiful women. Their first rounds of editing helped me make sense of the things in my head that I couldn't seem to get onto paper. They laughed with me, they cried with me, and cheered me over the finish line!

    Thank you to Jody Nash for taking my headshots and giving me so much love and confidence in front of your camera. Thank you for your friendship and thank you for your support.

    So many good friends have stood by me both in life and during this project and given me the love and courage to keep going. Donna Smith-Lathrope has cheered me on since the first day of kindergarten. Tonya Hutchison-Trapp has been my ride or die since high school. Lisa Fitzgerald-Bronson has listened to me laugh and cry for the last two decades. Freida James has propped me up when I didn't have any strength of my own. These women have been my family. From day one of this book, they have been there living it with me and believing in me. Thank you, from the very depths of my heart.

Introduction

Welcome to the craziness I call my life. Welcome to a story of sadness, loss, brokenness, betrayal, survival, enduring love, and faith. And right when it looks the darkest, you find a little humor. I have spent a long time thinking about writing my story. I always struggled with how to tell it. How do I tell a story that may never tie neatly into a bow? How do I speak about forgiveness and healing when I don't feel it every day? I have come to the conclusion that even if no one else ever reads this, I need to write it down for myself.

I want to write it down for my kids; I want them to look back over my life and know me. That is such a funny statement, because I've spent my whole life making sure that no one really knew me. I have gone to great lengths to only let people see the version of me I've created for them. That is my why. I want to be known. I want to quit hiding behind what I always believed were my flaws because that is who I am. I am a beautiful mess who has finally come to the realization that hiding parts of me will always make me feel less. I am not less. I am an ever-evolving portrayal of the battles I've won, the battles I've lost, and the ones I've decided to run from. Love me or hate me, I want to be known for who I really am.

Pamela Chastain

I am a survivor. In my life I have been a victim of circumstances that could have defined me. I have been a victim of childhood sexual abuse, a victim of severe emotional abuse, and a victim of domestic abuse. I have lost almost everyone close to me in my immediate family. I have survived through three failed marriages, and I've raised my three children on my own until now. Each circumstance has shaped me into the person I choose to be today. I choose to love unconditionally, and not let the people who hurt me define me.

I no longer run from a single one of those scars; I embrace them. Those scars have made me a better mother, a better wife, a better friend, and a better person. I no longer get up and look in the mirror to prepare for battle as I start my day. I look in the mirror and see a reflection of a woman who is loved, and most importantly, a woman who loves who she sees, flaws and all.

Finally Finding Bliss

So, let's start this story with where I am now. Telling this story reminds me of the *Lost* series on television. I loved this series (at least in the beginning), because they were all on a plane, and we knew tragedy was about to hit. Every one of those people had a story. How they got there would be woven into the storylines and this retrospective way of telling their backstories while dealing with the tragedies ahead fascinated me. I am writing this book as a 46-year-old happily married woman. Is this my first marriage? Well, no. Is it my second marriage? Well, sadly no. Is it my third? No again. This would be my fourth and final marriage—I mean it this time. I do not intend on trying to rival Elizabeth Taylor. The ironic part is that I truly never intended to EVER get married. I never intended to have children. I never intended to put myself in a position to be hurt and disappointed by men. As you will see, I don't take my own advice well.

Alan Chastain

Alan and I met on April 10, 2015. We got engaged May 19, 2015 and married June 4, 2015. After my history with men and relationships, I am quite certain that everyone in my life thought I had finally cracked up. That is, until they sat in a room with Alan.

You see, I have shown a great tendency in the past to pick the exact opposite of what I need and want. (Don't even look at me like that. Some of you do it, too.) Whether consciously or subconsciously, I picked people who I knew would let me down. But because I had no expectations, I wouldn't get hurt, right? Well, obviously not, because I have spent most of my adult life in some type of therapy and in revolving failed relationships that left me with wounds so deep, I'm certain my innermost cells were exposed. Then, in walked this man who thought those wounds were a little sexy. His wounds were just as deep as mine. He loved me in a familiar way, the way a good father would. The way that feels like a warm blanket on a cold day. Oddly enough, I think he loved my flaws much more than the very few things I believed made me a good catch.

Between the two of us, we have eight children between the ages of 8 and 32. Although he is only nine years older than I am, he has a grandson the age of my youngest child. Odd, crazy and a little overwhelming when you contemplate blending two families that are each a hot mess on their own. He has four adult kids, and last year when we started this roller coaster, we had four children at home. When we married, I had not even met all of his adult children. Stop the judging! Also, his mother referred to me as "the Devil" and wouldn't speak to either of us. Just in case the sweet warm-blanket comment from earlier had you jealous, I thought I would let you off the hook.

No, our life is not a bed of roses. In fact, one of the children in our brood, on any given day, either isn't talking to us or is ignoring our calls. Luckily, since there are so many, we don't have time to take it too seriously. Let's be very clear, I do not think anyone will hand me parenting awards after reading this book. I intend to be honest, and sometimes I have fallen short of what the "judgie" people will say is proper parenting. However, my children are loved. I guess that will count as their consolation prize for not being born to a more emotionally stable parent.

As I sit here typing, we have faced so much in these first two years. I am sitting here not working for the first time since my sixteenth birthday, my husband is facing open heart surgery this month, and my oldest will probably be deployed any minute by the Navy. If there is a time in my life that I should be struggling with my need to control things and be living in fear, it should be now, but I feel at peace. I feel like I am exactly where I am destined to be, and I feel more than ever that God is in complete control of where I am. I am not sure if this feeling is more because of my own journey or my husband's. I do know for certain that God has continued to "clear my plate" until I would listen to the voice in my heart telling me to quit running—to quit running not only from my past, but also my present. You see, I learned very early on to keep myself insanely stretched and busy. It kept all the feelings at bay. Well, my plate is as clear as God can make it, so I felt like I had to quit running, start remembering, and start typing.

Some of this may be difficult to read. Believe me, it has been difficult to type. I haven't invented anything important, I am not a multimillionaire, and I haven't done this gracefully. But what I have learned is that every single scar is part of a story where God is present, blessing me abundantly along the way by not only being a puzzle piece in someone else's life, but accepting that they were also a puzzle piece to my life. And with God, the pieces fit perfectly. I always felt my story would be a story of survival, but it is actually a story of being present and finding humor, while recognizing the gifts He gave me along the way. Alan Chastain is certainly one of the best and most touching ones. I couldn't be facing this laptop had God not put him in my life. He loves me enough to insist that I stay home and enjoy some peace and find my voice to tell my story, so here we go.

Stewie

Stewie may be a great place to start. Of course, I could write a book just about him alone. Maybe I will start another book about raising teenagers and call it *Did You See Satan?* Or even better *Did You See My Mental Breakdown?*

First of all, his name is Alec. Up until a year ago, I refused to even call him by a nickname because I love his name so much. He is named for my beloved sister, Alecia. Just saying her name brings such a confusion of emotions. I want to laugh, cry and sometimes crawl into a fetal position (just don't tell my therapist I admitted it). I was Alecia's birthday present when she was five years old. Back in the dark ages they couldn't tell parents whether they were having a girl or boy, so every single day of mom's pregnancy, Alecia prayed for a little sister. She was surrounded by brothers, kind of like a brother sandwich. My older brother, Damien, was a year older, and John was two years younger. So in reality it wasn't that she wanted a younger sister as much as she didn't want another brother. Well luckily (or unluckily) for her I was due to be born on her birthday. In Pamela fashion, I was late and we didn't get to share the exact same birthday. To say that I belonged to Alecia would be an understatement. I was her own living doll, from what I have heard anyway. She refused to let me

Who Did You See?

sleep in my own crib or bed and soon, we just got one big bed which we shared until she went to college. I don't want to delve too much into our childhood yet, so let's just say that when she went to college, she made trips home almost every weekend to pick me up and take me back with her. Being apart was too much for either of us to bear.

I had already flunked out of my first marriage and had jumped into a relationship with quite the "winner winner chicken dinner" of a second husband. (Be patient, my failures take a long time to explain). Regardless, I found myself in my second marriage, raising my stepson, because we had obtained emergency custody of him. We wanted a child of our own, but I was unable to get pregnant. My doctor put me on clomid, no luck. During one of my daily conversations with Alecia, I realized I was late. How late, you ask? Very late, like four months late, but when you are so disappointed time after time, you stop keeping track. Alecia told me to go, to run and get a pregnancy test. She stayed on the phone with me while we waited for the results. I was so nervous I held the stick upside down and thought it was broken, but she coached me through it and it was positive!

Two weeks later, tragedy struck. I don't think there are enough words to describe that day or to make you understand the impact that it had on my life. As my body was trying to adjust to all the hormonal changes of being with child, I couldn't keep anything down. On that day, May 30, 1997, I was so ill that I left work and went home to crawl into bed. My now ex-husband had turned the ringer off on the phone to make sure that I got some rest. I remember waking up startled from a dead sleep. Although I had no idea the ringer was off, I went running to the phone because I knew it was ringing. It was Rusty, my sister's husband. The minute I heard his voice, I knew something was wrong. I remember feeling alone for the first time in my life. I remember knowing that part of me was gone right at that moment.

Rusty told me that Alecia was at the hospital. He didn't want me to know how serious it was. I remember telling my husband all the way there that she was gone. Alecia had contracted meningococcal meningitis. No one could explain it at the time. I talked to Alecia every day, most often several times a day. I spoke with her the night before when she got home from teaching her daughter's dance class. She said she felt like she had pulled something in her back. I called that morning to check on her and remember Rusty telling me she thought she had the flu. He was going to keep the kids quiet and let her rest.

Who Did You See?

That afternoon, Rusty heard her in the bathroom running a bath and thought she must be feeling better. He was wrong. He found her purple and losing consciousness, so he lovingly wrapped her in the comforter from their bed and rushed her to the hospital. But she was gone. She was taken from three beautiful children who adored her, a husband who was just smitten and so in love with her, and from me, the one who loved her like no other. When I got to the hospital, they didn't have to tell me that she was gone, I knew it. I remember the mumblings of people saying, "she is here." I remember people not being able to look me in the eye and avoiding my questions. I remember being as gone as our Alecia was gone. Because of my pregnancy, they wouldn't let me see her or say my goodbye.

I remember going back to the house with Rusty and telling the children. The next few days are hard to recall. I just knew there was a deep hole left in my soul and nothing would ever be able to fill it. The days came and went but didn't seem like reality. I felt like I was trapped in someone else's body. I remember crying violently in bed and then hearing her name on CNN. They were reporting about a mother from Lebanon, Tennessee who had died. My crying stopped, but my heart was broken all over again hearing her name and the story as they reported it. There had not been any reported cases of meningococcal meningitis in Wilson County, Tennessee, in over a decade. No one understood or could explain how this happened. Although I am uncertain of a lot of things, I can tell you with absolute certainty that had I not been pregnant, I would not be here. Had God not surprised me two weeks earlier--to the day-- with that pregnancy, I would not have summoned the strength to put one foot in front of the other. But in His infinite wisdom and timing, God gave me Alec. He was my gift and one of many that remind me daily that God never leaves us, is always here with me, and loves me in spite of my life experiences telling me otherwise. So, what other name could this special gift have but one that represented unconditional love and her acceptance of my true self, a name symbolic of my dear sister Alecia?

    I hope to have an opportunity to write many more stories about Alec and my adventures, and trust me, there are enough for a few novels of the road that Alec and I have walked together. What I want you to know without a doubt is that Alec was a gift to me—you'll never convince me otherwise. God knew what He was taking from me, and although Alecia's time was done, He replaced in my womb the strength and promise of love that could and would carry me forward.

Who Did You See?

Alec has always been the life of the party, even when no one else knew there was a party going on. He was breastfed way too long, was a Momma's boy of epic proportion, and can have people wrapped around his finger while simultaneously wanting to slam their fists through a door. In other words, he is one of my favorite people on the planet. I think a lot of Alec's journey may be his story to tell, but what I can tell you is that the idea you have that your children won't bear your wounds rarely happens. Although his wounds are different, they are certainly deep and have formed who he is today. Me, I was dealing with my own demons and made many bad choices, like choosing his father. But, I know now that this was part of shaping us both. I chose his father knowing he would not be who I needed him to be. Unluckily, now that has extended to his children and I have carried that guilt as my own cross.

Alec is now an adult and is serving his country honorably in the Navy. I don't doubt he will find his way. How many of us stay on the path of healing continuously? It is a long and meandering road and he will have to learn to maneuver it just like I am doing. He has made me proud in so many ways, but the thing that makes me most proud is his ability to truly love people for who they are. Important to note—not who he wants or needs them to be, but who they are. He is learning to limit their ability to hurt him (as we know that is a work in progress) but manages to still love them.

    He has gone through periods of ignoring his father, refusing to see his father, and living temporarily with his father. He has come to terms with the relationship he has now with his father. For so many years he let all those difficult situations wind him up into destructive behavior. Now he is learning to recognize them, and that pleases me greatly. I could write a million chapters about raising him and what a gift he is to me and the people around him. However, for this story, I want you to understand what a present he was to me. He represents for me a living and breathing representation that I was on God's mind and heart. I choose to believe that He gave me the opportunity to have and raise Alec as a constant reminder that He not only loves me, but that He trusted me with such a special gift. For someone who feels broken and unworthy, God knew me well enough to know that I would find a way to love him with my whole heart.

    Now that you are feeling good about me as a parent, I will tell you where his nickname comes from. Alec would definitely be described by his friends as a wild child, to say the least. I had hoped that he would sail through his teen years without experimenting with drugs and alcohol. Somewhere, that request was misunderstood, and interpreted as a reason to experiment with all of it. One of those particularly wild nights would be his junior prom. I'll spare you the details, although pretty funny. Alec slept the majority of the following day, but when he came downstairs, in one of the funniest disheveled states I have ever seen, we kept looking and laughing, knowing he reminded us of something. While we sat and laughed at his stories, his stepbrother (while giggling uncontrollably), sent us all a picture of Stu from the Hangover movie. Other than still having his front tooth, he absolutely could have passed for his body double. Hence, from that day forward, he has been "Stewie." He even refers to himself as Stewie now.

    I wish that his road had been easier. I wish he had kept all those diversions out of his path. I wish he had not come from a broken home. However, he, like me, is a quilt made up of all those patches. He has chosen to make them just part of his story, but they do not define him.

Pamela Chastain

My Life Rope

After Alecia died in 1997, and Alec was born in 1998, I dove headfirst into raising Alec, trying my best to protect him from the challenging dynamics of my marriage. Additionally, I also did my best to be there for Alecia's three children who were struggling daily with the loss of their mother. Although I felt like half of me died with my sister, the kids and Alec kept making me pull up my bootstraps and put one foot in front of the other. I presented a happy front to anyone who didn't look very closely. As far as anyone knew, I was happily married and thriving, while underneath the surface I felt like a piece of me was dying every day.

I am the baby of four children. Damien, the oldest, was six years older than me. Alecia was five years older than me, and John was three years older than me. Without delving completely into the details now, Alecia, John and I were all sexually abused by our oldest brother, Damien. It made us abnormally close and dependent on each other and we each handled it very differently. John handled it as do a lot of survivors of sexual abuse—he became very self-destructive. But to know John was to be in love with John. He was forever an optimist and truly saw the beauty in everyone other than himself. Just saying his name brings a smile to my face and memories can rush through me like

Who Did You See?

a wave. John struggled with addiction, but eventually found peace. After some time, he even found love with his partner, Dean, and lived in Chattanooga.

John had a habit of calling me when he was at his worst and it always ended up with me lecturing him about why he was in that state. I would tell him that he can't let Damien win. It always felt like this never-ending cycle of him calling drunk just for me to end up yelling at him. The last time I spoke with John, he called and could barely speak he was so drunk. I don't remember what all was said, but I remember feeling something snap in me. With my marriage, the kids, my family, and all the stress and my own depression, I just didn't want to "mother him" that day. A week later on December 4, 2000, he called to wish me happy birthday and I didn't answer the phone. I was still irritated and a little scared to answer for fear he may be in a bad state again. That is one of the days I would trade any amount of money to go back to and pick up the phone. The following week, on December 11, 2000 John died. John and his partner Dean had gone to a Christmas party and had just gotten home. He turned to say something to Dean and dropped. Dean was an EMT and after calling 911, he tried CPR but no one could get John back. He had a massive brain aneurysm. Again, those next few days are a blur to me. I remember having to call Mom and Dad. I gathered the kids' things and drove to Chattanooga. Most of all, I remember sitting by his bedside. They made us wait for 24 hours to make sure there was no brain activity. I vividly remember the sounds of the machines that were breathing for him and I remember every time something made a sound thinking that maybe he was breathing. I knew he wasn't, but I just couldn't believe that I was never going to see his beautiful smile again. Another of the last few people who really knew me, and knew how badly I was broken, was gone. I wouldn't get any more of those calls that I dreaded, but I wouldn't ever get to enjoy one of his full belly laughs. And now, I would never, ever be the same again. This death changed me in a way that Alecia's had not.

    I had to arrange for his body to be brought home, and I planned another funeral. I don't even know how to explain what I was feeling at the funeral, or the next few weeks that followed. "Numb" does not even come close to describe it. I went from feeling like part of me was dying, to feeling like I was dragging my own dead corpse through my daily life. I do, however, remember three weeks after John's death waking up and knowing he was with me. I walked out onto the deck of our house and sat on the stairs and had a talk with him. I told him how sorry I was that I had

Who Did You See?

not been there for him the way that I should have been. The wind was blowing, and I distinctly heard him tell me to hold on because God was going to fill my heart back up in a way that I would have no more room to mourn him. I could see his smile. I hugged him and smelled that familiar 80's cologne he refused to quit wearing.

Several months passed and the depression that came over me was so severe that I cannot tell you how I managed to press on. I quit sleeping, and began having panic attacks that were so severe, I would find myself on the side of the road throwing up uncontrollably. I would go into work every day, pull the blinds down in my office and cry. I would stop soon enough so that I could put cold packs on my eyes and re-do my makeup so that the kids wouldn't know when I got home. I worked for a medical placement company. They rented an office from a corporate suite rental company. One day the assistant manager stopped me to meet her best friend. I stopped and spoke to her for a minute and proceeded to my office to pull my blinds and cry. When I saw her later she explained that her friend, Lindsay, was a counselor and that she wanted me to have her number. When I tell you that God has spoken to me through people at the right time, at the exact right moment, this is one of those times. That day, they saved my life. I can promise you that I was too scared and lost to seek help for myself and that deep hole was swallowing me. Because my life was in such chaos, and I had so many people depending on me, they took me in. When I say they took me in, I mean they literally took me into their house. They prayed over me, they counseled me, they gave me space to breathe and sleep, and ultimately saved my life.

I had an experience staying with the two of them that I did not know how to explain to anyone. It was such a personal experience that I wasn't sure I ever wanted to share it. I know you probably feel a little lost in this story. Please hang in there and know that I will bare my soul. It's a very long and complicated story. What I will say for now, is that I didn't have the time for a nervous breakdown. I had never discussed or dealt with the abuse, or the long line of things that had been done to me up to this point. I had spent my entire life completely internalizing everything. I was so insistent that I was okay. I actually got up every morning and looked in the mirror to prepare for battle. I had this ridiculous idea that if I presented to everyone that I was okay and beyond reproach, with all my balls constantly in the air, that no one would look closely enough at what an absolute disaster I truly was.

When John died and I hit that wall, I couldn't pull off the facade anymore. I couldn't even remotely pretend that I could cope. I was unable to take care of myself, much less all of the people depending on me. If they had not taken me in and given me the time to catch my breath in a safe place, I truly believe I would not have made it. During that time, I slept, I read, I prayed, I talked, I cried, I laughed, and for the first time in a long time, I didn't feel the pressure of having to perform for everyone. There was no expectation to do anything other than breathe, rest, and heal.

On the last Sunday I was there, they asked if they could anoint and pray over me. I grew up in a very traditional Southern Baptist upbringing. I went to a church where you said Amen at structured appropriate times, and on Sunday, you only brought your best to Jesus. The idea of anything like this was foreign to me, but I knew if there was anyone I could trust it was these women. They took oil and anointed me, laid their hands on me, and began to pray. I couldn't tell you a single thing they prayed for, but I could feel how much they loved me.

Praise and worship music was playing and when I laid back on the couch, I began to feel light. I wasn't sure if I was sick or feeling faint, but I shut my eyes and I am not sure if I can find the words to explain what happened to me. I felt a peace fall over me. I felt a combination of feeling light as a feather but weighted down as if I was anchored to the couch. I began to see memories, like I was asleep, but fully awake. For years I had purposely pushed all memories of Alecia and John completely out of my mind and they were suddenly flooding through me, wave after wave. All good memories; all good times we shared. They were there with me. I could smell John's cologne and I could hear Alecia whispering to me like she did when we played games at night in bed. They reminded me they were always in my heart if I could just push past the pain of loss and remember how much we shared. That time, and particularly that day, was another gift. God put Lindsay and Sandy in my life. He was reminding me again that I wasn't alone, that I was worthy, even if I didn't feel like I was.

When I had to leave the safety of their house and face the chaos back in my own life, I tried very hard to hold onto the peace I found there. It was short-lived. It didn't take many couples therapy sessions to realize that the biggest and most difficult factor in my life was my marriage. Therapy became a band-aid, or maybe a better description is an emergency triage. I would go in at the point of falling into a million pieces. We would gather a few of the pieces, put them back on, and I would go home to face my life that was spiraling out of control.

In July 2002 my husband and I decided to take a quick trip to Florida by ourselves. We had never gotten away without the kids and traveled to Destin for a quick trip. What we brought back from that trip would be the blessing that John told me was coming.

Pamela Chastain

Krista Grace

As I have said too many times already, each one of my precious children are truly gifts from God. However, this one came in extra-special wrapping. Krista is an amazing mixture of pure sweetness and absolute spunk. She can make me smile bigger, laugh harder, and cry more than anyone else in my life at just the thought of her storytelling. She hates when anyone calls her my Mini-Me and refuses to believe that she looks like me or has any of my traits. However, truth be told, she is such an improved version of me, it would almost be insulting to make the comparison.

Krista came roaring into my life on May 20, 2003 and I am not sure if anything could have prepared me for how she stole my heart the first time I looked into her engaging eyes. She was absolutely the most beautiful thing I had ever seen. She was born with the longest eyelashes (which she still has today) and was such a happy baby. Krista Grace was the epitome of everything I had ever wanted in a little baby girl, and it scared the literal hell out of me. I found myself waking up in the middle of the night in a panic and rushing to her room. Memories of my abuse would come flooding back in the still hours of the night, hearing his breathing outside my door. The panic I felt to protect this little girl had my mind playing tricks on me, convinced he was in the house. I was nursing Krista so I was up with her at night, but I found myself sitting beside her crib, paralyzed and scared to leave her alone.

To make things even more difficult, my brother Damien and his family moved to our small town. He was now right down the road from our family. Damien's children attended the same elementary school as ours and his son played ball in the same baseball league. Of all places in the state of Tennessee, he had to be near me and my family. I could not get away from him. He was at the school when I dropped off the kids, at the store when I was buying groceries, at the ball field when my children were playing, and now he was haunting me in my sleep. Why could I not find the peace I had found during my time away with Lindsay? Peace of any measure was eluding me, so I was not sleeping. These feelings were too familiar—that feeling of drowning, gasping for air to get through the day. Not only could I not go back there, I didn't want to. I may have been trapped in a horrible marriage, but I had these two amazing children! I had proof that God knew I wasn't too broken. He trusted me with these amazing souls and they needed me to keep myself together.

Every time I felt like I was at the end of my rope, Krista's infectious smile penetrated my soul.

She has always had this beautiful and huge personality. From the very beginning, she had a way of wrapping everyone around her pinky finger. It wasn't by being demanding or acting up, or even being especially sweet. Krista could command a room from the time she could walk. There are many stories I could share about Krista, I have chosen two that I feel really capture her persona.

Krista was always stuck to my side like glue and was definitely my little Barbie doll. She loved to be dressed up, wanted her hair done, and I could not keep her out of my nail polish and make-up. One afternoon after she was quite pleased with her "look" (at the age of 4), I asked her what she wanted to be when she grew up, to which she responded, "I want to be beautiful." To be honest, it was one of those parenting moments where I thought, "Am I not telling her how beautiful and wonderful she is enough?" When I told her that she was already beautiful and I knew she would grow up and be so smart and so beautiful, she didn't let me finish because she started crying uncontrollably. She looked me square in the face and said, "No, Mom, I don't want to be smart. I want to be beautiful, and you can't be both!" Being quite alarmed, I said, "Krista, of course you can!" Her response, "No Mom, you can't. You are just smart now." She was on to a new adventure and I never had time to lick my wounds. Her ability to be both sweet and direct has been with her from the beginning. The boys were always annoyed with my need to dress them up and show them off—not Krista. She has always loved nothing better than to be all dolled up, but on her own terms.

Of all my children, not a single time did I ever get called to school by the principal—until Krista. The first week of Kindergarten, Krista started complaining about a boy at school who was getting in her personal space. He wouldn't leave her alone in class, at lunch, or on the bus. I kept reassuring her that there would be those people in her life, just to ignore him and he would get bored eventually. Well, the principal of the school rang me and was trying not to laugh. She didn't know the whole story, but considering my stepson and Alec had both gotten through their elementary years without visiting her office, she found it funny that she was calling me about Krista. There had been an issue in the lunchroom, and she wanted me to come to the school. Krista had apparently had enough that day. The boy was standing behind her in line and kept poking her. She said that she asked him several times to stop touching her and every time he poked her harder. Well, Krista lost it. Not only did she mow him over like a linebacker, she stood over him taunting him. She stood over him yelling, "Cry harder, cry harder you little baby." We all learned a lot about Krista that day as she sat there in the Principal's office straight up in her chair and looked her straight in the face and said, "surely you aren't angry with me—I gave him more than one warning." She never shed a tear until we got home and no one could see her.

This moment will always represent the essence of Krista to me, and even funnier, it is such a snapshot of her mother. I had a similar moment in Kindergarten with a boy. Sam, for some reason, was obsessed with me. Listen, he was. He wouldn't leave me alone. He followed me around the class, the playground, insisted on trying to sit with me at lunch. One day, like Krista, I had enough when he put those nasty germy lips on my cheek while we were on the playground. I snapped, quite like Krista, and hit him so hard he tumbled down the hill on the playground end over end. My Dad was called, and for years he re-told that story laughing and almost proud about how I sat in the chair righteously angry that I was the one in trouble. My Dad laughed at the whole story, grabbed me up and kissed me on the forehead and took me for ice cream. He was proud of me for taking up for myself, and I wish I had told him the truth about all the things going on at home that day. That day, like all the days to follow, I wanted him to look at me like he did that day, proudly.

Who Did You See?

So now this princess is about to turn 14 and is going into high school, which is crazy to think about. Facing the reality of having so few years with her left and talking to her about what lies ahead is another reason I think I felt the pull to write this book. Making the transition from middle to high school was such a turning point for me. Like Alec, Krista carries wounds from growing up with divorced parents. She carries anger with me, her dad, and with the disappointment that life is harder for her than for her friends who come from what she believes are "ideal" homes. Which is exactly how I felt, so I get her. Going into that transition, I wanted so badly to feel "normal" and I felt like an absolute freak show. I started down a path that led me to decisions which haunt me still today. I want more for her. I don't want her to feel a need to morph into what others want from her or hide who she is to make anyone else happy.

Isn't that the real challenge for girls? That gets to the very idea of why I titled this book Who Did You See? Women are expected to be strong yet soft, smart yet understanding, I always assumed that I struggled so hard because of the abuse, but this is one of the few things that I know now is the same for all girls. We feel a need to shield what we perceive as flaws and show people a version of ourselves that we think will make us more accepted. I always saw Krista as this beautiful little firecracker who would never struggle with the need to compromise how she sees herself. She would be so loved and understood that she would love who she is, flaws and all. Unfortunately, this is something I can't give to her. I know now that I have to love her enough to sit on the sidelines and watch her struggle with the exact same issues that I blamed on my abuse. I see her change into a different version of herself and struggle with her self-image, all the while thinking about that stubborn and beautiful child so comfortable in her own skin.

I pray every day that she will never lose herself in her daily walk. I know that life is going to continue to throw her obstacles and I pray that she always remembers the little girl who knew that she deserved to be respected by that little boy who wasn't listening to her warning. I pray she learns to handle it better, but hey, she is my child with my temper...

My Warrior

Many of you reading this will question, "Where was your father?" How did this happen in a Christian home where everyone saw us as an ideal Southern Baptist family? Well, it happens just as often in homes like mine as any other place. My perspective on my story has certainly changed as I have become an adult, struggled with own mistakes, struggled with parenting, and juggled my own baggage. My parents, just like me, did things wrong—and right—and found themselves making their way through parenting knowing that they wanted better for their own children than what they came from. In many ways, we had exactly that. In other ways, it was just as bad as what they experienced.

My father was a warrior. He lived his life by a code that he set. If you didn't like it or understand it, he didn't care. He didn't need anyone's approval. He did, however, love the people in his life with a strong, steady and irreplaceable love. There were no male leaders in his life from which he could mirror how to be a father. He came from a place that was so horrific, he left home at an early age to escape the abuse. Yet, somehow he found a way to instill a strength and deep love for me—without it, I could NOT have survived.

My father has a story that would fill many pages of his own novel. His story of strength and endurance would put most men to shame. He served his country honorably until he had a bad parachute jump and broke his back and neck in three places. He found himself in a hospital being told that he would never walk again and was being medically discharged from the army. He was newly married with his first child on the way. This was a man who, at this time in his life, didn't believe in God. If there was a God, my dad felt that He was certainly angry with him.

While still in the hospital, he picked up a paintbrush and realized the gift that God had given him. My father took an art class and found his calling. He was an amazing artist and had a way to provide for the family he adored. Even more importantly, he never gave up, and he believed that he would be just as strong as he was before. He left that hospital walking on his own, and never looked back. Although he didn't know it at the time, it was the first step in finding the relationship with God that sustained him through the rest of his years.

The story of how he finally found his faith still makes me laugh. The similarities between my father and me are remarkable. God never gives up on any of us, but with some of us, he really has to show up "where we are" and speak to us "how we will listen." After my father was discharged from the army, my parents relocated to Madison, Tennessee. My mom found a church and started bringing her children to church every Sunday. My father didn't understand it. He didn't understand why anyone would get up on a weekend morning, struggle with getting the kids ready, and drag them to church.

My father was convinced the only reason my mom would do that was to see another man. He believed she must be having an affair with someone at church. So, one Sunday morning he went with her. He went with her to see who she was seeing there. What he found was that God was there waiting for him. God was there waiting to be the father to him that he never had. God was there waiting to speak softly in his ear and tell him that he WAS worth saving. God was there anxiously waiting to show him that there is nothing that is beyond forgiveness. That moment when my father found God waiting there changed all of our lives. When he found God, it changed everything about who he chose to be from that day forward. He loved God with a fierceness that was shocking to people. I believe it showed him how to love all of us.

Pamela Chastain

Becoming A Real Father

We didn't come from much and we didn't have a lot. However, because of the change in my father, I did have an irreplaceable love. I was the baby, his little Puddin', and he adored me. I wouldn't say that I could do no wrong, because he was hard on me when he needed to be. I will say, he didn't need to be hard on me very often. I couldn't stand my father being upset with me. My father had the most expressive green eyes. They remind me now of my own, changing colors based on my mood. When he was angry, they were a very deep green. He scowled when he was angry, much like I see myself doing now that I am older. When he was angry and his eyes were intensely green, I felt like he could see behind my mask. I couldn't have that. I needed him to see only what I allowed, so that I could have him look at me with softness and acceptance. I needed that from him, and I gave up having an "honest" relationship with him to have it. As a child, I didn't understand that I was compromising having real protection from him by hiding what was happening to me.

I received a single spanking growing up. Yes, just one. I am not saying that I didn't need more than one, I just received only one. My parents put me in private dance lessons at the age of four. My father was a deacon in the church, a Southern

Who Did You See?

Baptist Church, where dancing was forbidden. He was willing to deal with the backlash at church because he loved to see me dance. The irony of knowing that my father was willing to stand up for me may be one of the reasons why I loved dancing so fiercely. I didn't feel strong enough to share what else was going on but clung to the fact that he was protecting me.

My mother is a very long story to write about. Although she has some amazing qualities, she is difficult to love. My Father adored her. I don't believe he was oblivious to her flaws but loved her with such pure adoration in spite of them. He always credited her for leading him to church to find his faith, and I always believed that is why he ignored her shortcomings. He loved all of us that way.

Being the youngest, I had a special relationship with my father. He loved to tell people that at four years old I could tell you all the moving parts to a jet engine. I certainly cannot now, and I certainly don't remember that, but if my father was interested in something, I was interested in that same thing. He had no idea of the abuse that was going on under his roof. He had no idea that his wife, who he adored so much, knew and made the choice to hide it from him and everyone else. He was oblivious to it for many, many years and because of that I eventually just didn't want him to know. I was not tainted in his eyes. I am not sure now if I wanted to protect him, or my own image in his eyes. Maybe both. I tell you all of this so you have a sense of the power this man held in our family, even though he wasn't in control of what was going on in his own home.

My father was diagnosed with prostate cancer the first time in between the deaths of my sister and my brother. He was still working full time and although they told him it was a large, aggressive tumor, they felt they could get it all with surgery alone. My father hated the idea of chemotherapy and radiation, so he was happy with that plan. Ultimately, that was probably the decision that killed him. He had the surgery but continued to battle it time after time until it took his life in 2007. During his last few months with us, we decided to let him pass at home as he wanted. I watched this strong, stubbornly active man wither away in front of my eyes. In my many rants between the years of Alecia's and John's deaths and the imminent death of my father, I railed at God about how unfair it was that I didn't get to say goodbye to either Alecia or John. I would shake my fists at God about how painful it was to not have the opportunity to say my goodbyes to them. Well, like most things, I found out that I was wrong. It was much more painful to sit with my father every day and watch him turn into a shell of who he was.

My father was such a rare and amazing man, but I will never finish this book if I get sidetracked on all his complexities. On the outside he looked like a simple man, but he was anything but simple. It is important for you to know for now that he never lost his faith. He remained thankful for every single day, no matter the pain, no matter the hardships. It was another day to love me and my mother. It was another day to spend telling me stories and just enjoying each other's company. There was never this push between us in those last days to say last words, because we had been saying them every single day. There wasn't this need for him to make some lasting mark on my life because he had done it every single day. He was never angry at God for all he had been through; he was accepting. It was remarkable to watch this man in so much pain fight but not be angry.

My father stayed in his Lazy Boy chair up until the last 12 hours of his life. He told me during his struggle that I could not bring a hospital bed into his house. He knew the minute that he got into that bed, he would die. My Father's cancer had become metastatic and it was literally eating away the bones in both his spinal column and his ribs. To complicate the matter, he was allergic to all the "big guns" that would help with his pain, like Morphine and Dilaudid. We had to be inventive with a series of painkillers to try to make him comfortable. We could never really get him pain-free because we couldn't get him comfortable at home without the stronger medicines.

During one of the times we called an ambulance to transport him to the hospital because his pain was out of control, he kept having a recurring dream about my next blessing. He would wake up startled from a deep sleep with stories of this beautiful boy with his own green eyes and long curly hair. He would tell me of this smile that would make his soul full and how much this boy loved me. I kept telling him that he was remembering Alec as a little boy and he would just belly laugh and say, "No Pam. I can't stand your husband but thank goodness you didn't listen and went back. This one, this one is going to have you wrapped like you do me." I think about those moments a lot now, looking into that gift's beautiful eyes that mirror my father's. He was right—Jack does have me wrapped utterly and completely around his pinky finger.

We lost my father on October 21, 2007, a week before his 70th birthday. He went quietly at home and was finally at peace. About 12 hours prior, he had let us bring in a hospital bed, and we put him on Methadone which immediately eliminated his pain. He slept soundly, finally. After sleeping almost 11 hours, he woke up and looked straight into my eyes. He called me Puddin' and told me he had loved me since the first time he saw me and that he was glad I was the one with him. He reminded me that I was strong and I deserved more than what I had been choosing. He wanted me to do better. He also asked the most difficult thing he could ask of me, to take care of my mother for him. I think he knew what I would have to do, and I think he held on and fought as hard as he did because of that. My mother and I simply have never liked each other. She made it very clear she never wanted a fourth child, and to say that our relationship was difficult would be an understatement. I wouldn't take on that chore of taking her in for anyone else but my father. He fell back asleep and was gone in less than an hour. He passed just like he had lived his life, with dignity, and reminding me how much I was loved right up until the very end.

Pamela Chastain

Little Jack

After Daddy passed, I continued to struggle with his loss as well as with my overwhelming life. I was drowning even deeper into depression and my marriage was a bigger disaster every single day. We were unhappy, disastrously unhappy, and our lives had gotten caught up in a saga that is a narrative all by itself. In my heart, I knew we shouldn't have any more children, but I had put off getting the procedure done. I finally scheduled it at a client's office; I was the last procedure for the day. As I sat in a back office doing her billing, a nurse kept asking me to take a pregnancy test. It annoyed me and I remember thinking that it was a ridiculous waste of time and supplies, but I relented. The next few hours became a blur like many others in my life. I remember the nurse and doctor coming into my office, shutting the door and asking if I was late for my period. Well you guessed it, I was pregnant. Six pregnancy tests later, and more than an hour crying in the bathroom and I picked up my boot straps and headed to share the good news with my estranged husband.

We kept pretending to the outside world that our marriage would make it, and we brought little Jack into the world on December 18, 2008. It was a very difficult pregnancy, complicated even more by the situation at home, but Little Jack had my absolute devotion the minute I saw his beautiful face and held his sweet little hand. It was an even more special day for me because my sister's oldest was in the delivery room with me. Asia cheered me on, while trying not to pass out. I was 38 years old, had a newborn, two other children of my own, my step-son, and my sister's three kids. My marriage was killing me, and I was still mourning the loss of my father, my brother, and my sister. As difficult and overwhelming as all of that was, I was given another visible reminder that God was giving me just as much as he was taking from me.

Jack is exactly what my father promised he would be. He is quietly strong like my father. He doesn't have a lot to say, but when he does, you know he has been thinking it through. He doesn't like a lot of people around him, because he says people get on his nerves (just like my father felt), and the people he does let in he loves with the same passion that my father did. Jack is absolutely the exact opposite from his brother and sister in a million ways. Alec and Krista have always had these huge personalities and have never met a stranger. Jack is so funny and so smart, but not many people get to see that side of him. To say he is shy is an understatement.

I have often wondered if not having memories of his father and me together makes being the child of divorce easier or more difficult. I know that he will have his own struggles, but I don't see him struggle the way Krista and Alec have. He has always just been "my" son, attached to my hip, and the biggest mama's boy ever. I worry about his ability to make lasting relationships and have attachments to people. He shows no real desire to make a lot of friends. As long as he has one friend he doesn't have a need for others, and he only seems to have time for them on his own terms. He is the sweetest boy ever, doesn't sound like it, but he is. He is the first to want to write a note or draw a picture for anyone having a bad day or for a special occasion. Just don't ask him to give it to them.

Jack doesn't want to play ball, refuses sleepovers, and if you ask him about girlfriends, he says, "No, I only love my Mommy." Although it makes my heart full that he feels so loved, I worry all the time what would happen to Jack if I wasn't here. I have learned the hard way that we aren't promised more time, and I am not sure how Jack would survive without me.

What I have found with this last child is that I have gotten to enjoy him much more. I haven't found myself sitting by his bedside in a panic as I did with Krista or worrying about every single sniffle like it was the plague, which I did with Alec.

Who Did You See?

I am not sure if that is a testament to where I am emotionally or if it is simply because I now recognize my inability to control anything in our lives. I enjoy not just Jack more, but all three of them.

I recognize how much they reflect the people I have lost. Don't misunderstand me—no one could replace who I have lost. I don't think God replaced them for me. I do believe God knows my very soul so well that He knew that loving the people around me gives me purpose. Loving them would make me get up every day no matter how sad and mournful I became.

I believe God loved me enough to give my children gifts that would serve them just like they did for my sister, brother, and father. In writing this book I have spent so much time reflecting on them and I hadn't realized until now that when I talk about how Alec loves people, it is in the same amazing way that Alecia loved everyone around her. One of the things I miss most is John's beautiful voice. No one in our family could carry a tune in a bucket, but John had this amazing husky voice that could touch my soul. Guess what—so does Krista. She has a voice that makes my heart feel at peace. It sounds familiar. As I said before, Jack is quietly strong like my father and always seems to find his way to art to soothe himself or someone else, just like my father. All three of them live on, not as replacements, but in people who remind us all that the impact we leave on the lives of the people around us is everlasting.

Shame

So now comes the test for me. I can write all day long about how much I love my children. I can write about these people that were taken from me way too soon and how much I still miss them. The kicker is, can I really tell all of you "my story?" You see, when I told you about my therapist, what I didn't tell you is that in more than a decade of therapy I never found my voice to talk about the abuse that happened to me. I truly believed I wouldn't come out of it if I went back there. Over the years, I have heard so many stories that were worse than mine. So many people have endured so much worse than I experienced. So why did I believe I wasn't strong enough? I still struggle with this question. I think anyone who has ever known me would describe me as strong, possibly one of the strongest people they know. I think this struggle is part of a much deeper struggle with what I believe to be true about who I am. I barely go beyond the surface when I am dealing with an emotion that bubbles up related to any of these things, and then I go about my daily life putting the emotions back in their secure hiding place.

When I think about the things that happened to me as a child, I feel shame. I feel shame that I can't tell you many memories from my childhood because I have blocked so much of it out of my mind. I remember specific events that happened, and I don't think it is necessary for you to know details, but I want you to know that I don't remember a part of my childhood that isn't tainted by the memories of what my brother did to me. I think that it feels shameful to me because most of my family is gone. I don't have the luxury of going to a family holiday or reunion and asking questions to jar my memory to share with my own kids. I can't call Alecia and John and ask, "Hey, you remember when?" This feels like another betrayal, another battle my older brother won and took from me.

    My kids have a very big family on their dad's side. They have cousins, aunts, uncles, and grandparents. They have large family get-togethers and share memories. When Richard and I were married, these were horribly difficult for me. Often, I would find myself in the bathroom crying, which was met with anger by Richard and his family. I was annoying to them after the first year of my mourning. They were never big fans of me anyway, so it was another time in my life that I felt shut out or different. Now, whether accurate or inaccurate, my kids feel like they are disliked by his family because they are my children. My inability to share a family with them where they feel loved and accepted is one of the hardest things for me at the holidays. Not just for me, but more for the loss of what could have been the greatest joy of their lives.

Now, I know it isn't my brother's fault that they aren't here. I am not blaming him for that, but the shame of closing my mind to the happy memories because it was more important for him to take my voice as a child is completely and utterly his fault.

I feel shame because I was not brave enough to tell someone what was happening to me. I wasn't a wallflower who sat on the sidelines without friends or adult role models. I was the exact opposite. I had plenty of people in my life who I knew loved me. Had I asked for help, I know they would have heard me. I feel immense shame that I didn't tell any of them. For as long as I can remember, I developed this shield made up of all the things that I believed they wanted to see of me and my family. I hid all the pain and brokenness by being more than what anyone would expect from someone that was hurting. From early on, I knew that was how to keep anyone from looking too closely. I would move on to someone else who needed my attention because I acted like I had it all together.

I could read at the age of 4, so when I went to Kindergarten, I read books to the class instead of learning to read at school. Since that was expected of me now, I always had to make A's because if I made a B, someone would want to know why or what was wrong. When I wanted to be a cheerleader, I felt like it was expected that I would be in charge, so I had to be Captain. I spent so much of my childhood worrying and trying to invent this person who I wanted people to see that I let those moments pass by without learning to "experience" them. I don't remember the things I want to remember because my focus was on everyone's expectations of me and my own survival.

The shame I feel for keeping quiet is something I will struggle with for a very long time because the sexual abuse instilled in me a deep feeling of insecurity, thereby hindering my ability to make sound decisions. I am always putting more time into questioning myself about whether I am making a decision from a "good place," rather than focusing on the decision itself. That mistake has haunted me more than anything else, and it is completely self-perpetuating. It is something that haunts me more than anything else because it affects every aspect of my life. This is why I couldn't stop the cycle of abuse in my own life.

The shame of keeping quiet begged so many questions in my mind. Was I more scared that they wouldn't believe me, or that they would? If they did believe me, what would that mean for my family? Would they take me from my parents? Would Alecia, John, and I still be able to be together? Would they believe that my father didn't know?

Who Did You See?

Most importantly, how would my father see me now? Would I still be precious and beautiful, or would I be damaged and broken? Would he forgive my mother for knowing and keeping quiet? Would they get divorced now and what would happen to all of us? If the state got involved, would they leave me with my mother who didn't like me? Those questions kept me from sleeping, from having attachments and relationships that I wanted to have, and they robbed me of ever feeling the security that my father believed he provided for us at home.

Believe it or not, there were even times in my life that I wondered if I was so broken that I didn't tell anyone because I somehow enjoyed it or wanted it. I kept those feelings buried deep, very deep, in a place that I could only go when I was so down and depressed that I couldn't fall any further. My default reaction is to always take responsibility, to blame myself when things go wrong. I never gave myself the grace that I gave everyone else, and the shame stayed buried so deeply because of it. The shame I felt was a wound that I never let heal because to bring it to light would require me to face it.

Power

    I struggled for a long time on what to title this chapter. One of the things I know to be true about sexual abuse is, it is rarely, if ever, about the act itself. It is almost always about having power over someone, or about feeling powerless yourself. It has taken me 46 years and the last few months of pondering about this book to look at this from my brother's place. One of the times that I ran into Damien at Walmart after Alecia's death, I confronted him about what he had done. I rounded the corner of a grocery aisle and just about ran directly into his shopping cart. Normally, when I would see him in a store, I would leave immediately. I would feel my heart rate start to increase, I would taste the vomit in my mouth, and I would run from the store. I would find myself by my car throwing up and crying and angry with myself for being such a coward.

    This time was different. I had felt a growing anger inside of me and I looked up into the face that had brought so much fear into our lives. I asked him how he lived with himself now that she was gone and that he could never tell her he was sorry. I remember telling him she was different, that she would have forgiven him, because she just wanted to put it all behind her, unlike me. He said two very important things before I watched him

Who Did You See?

walk away. First, he looked deep into my eyes, curled a half smile with his lips, and he told me that he didn't waste time feeling sorry for ANY mistakes that he made. He wasn't sorry, not even a little. Secondly, he said that wasn't true because Mom had told him that Alecia had long ago forgiven him and that it didn't affect her life. She was happy and settled and I was just looking for attention—like always.

I remember watching him walk away and feeling very dizzy. I left my shopping cart, went to my car and just sat there. I felt completely and utterly powerless. I am unsure how long I sat there, but I eventually drove home and didn't tell anyone for a long time what had happened. This particular memory haunts me. Let's start with what he said first. That day, that painful confrontation proved to me that he wasn't sorry. He felt no remorse for anything that he did to us. He made a point to say that he didn't waste any time feeling sorry. He wanted me to feel like nothing again, he wanted to stand there one more time and make me feel small and vulnerable. I stood there as a grown woman and let him abuse me again. I did feel powerless.

Control can be a very scary but intoxicating feeling. I struggle for my need to control everyone and everything for exactly this reason. Once the abuse stopped, I made a vow to myself that I would never let anyone control me again. I used to talk about my life like a chessboard, constantly making sure all the pieces were in play where I needed them to be. I have found myself questioning how different that is from Damien's apparent need to control us or the circumstances at home for him. It is very different. However, it is not fair to the people in my life and it has done more damage to my soul instead of allowing it to heal. What made that little boy feel so out of control that he needed to control us? Is that even the reason why he did it? None of those questions entered my mind that day at Walmart because all I could think of was running.

    Power has always been an ongoing battle for me. I feel the tug to manipulate the people around me like my mother and brother did me. I want to hold the upper hand, so I very rarely let my guard down. It wasn't the idea of being in charge of a situation as much as knowing before a situation arose that I believed I knew what was going to happen—back to the myth of the chessboard. Just typing this makes the whole thing hilariously funny to me now. My life has been the worst example of keeping control. In fact, I have jokingly referred to my life as a series of unfortunate events. I can't think of many, if any, plans I have made that weren't turned upside down. It has been more like hanging on for dear life than charting my own course.

Who Did You See?

My therapist would describe my struggle as holding onto a two-handled coffee cup. I would come into a session completely at my wit's end, stomping my feet and yelling at God about my circumstances, and she would look at me with the funniest expression and say, "Pam how in the world are you giving God any power to bless you or help when you are holding on to that cup so tightly with both hands? Until you trust Him enough to put it down, or even let go with one hand, there isn't any room for him to get in there." I think about that talk a few times every week while enjoying my coffee. The need for power and the need to control come from the same place—a place that is filled with self-doubt and insecurity. Like any other character trait, it can be used for good or to inflict deep pain. I am guilty of both. Holding that mirror up to myself while typing this hurts. I just hope that someday the people in my life will love me in spite of that flaw and the pain I must have inflicted on them.

The last thing Damien said to me was that I was just looking for attention, like always. What an icing on the cake that was. He wanted me to believe what happened was my fault. I somehow was looking for attention and that is why he had abused me. It wasn't his fault; it was somehow mine. Whether he really believed that or not, he wanted to inflict another wound. He knew that would be another way to get a deep cut in before I inevitably ran away to lick my wounds. It worked; I ran away. I retreated back into the place where I felt helpless, wounded, and powerless. Sexual abuse is ultimately about taking someone's power away. I willingly gave him mine again and again because I hadn't found my voice yet. I have found my voice and taken back my power not by writing this book, but by choosing to love myself, flaws and all. I took back my power every day that I have chosen to live and love the people around me. I may have given it back to him at moments in my life, but each time I take it back is still another victory. There is much more power in having a life that is real and honest, and there is victory in loving who I am, just as I am. I do pray for Damien almost every day. Some days I have to forgive myself for not being able to, but I pray that he finds his own voice. I pray that he is able to forgive himself and find peace.

Anger

All of you are sitting there laughing right now and saying, "Well of course you are angry." Oddly enough, I have spent my entire life denying that fact, so I guess it took writing a book to admit the obvious. I think I always felt that admitting I was angry was somehow admitting defeat. It took almost 47 years to find strength in being vulnerable. At so many points in my life, I thought I was being vulnerable, but I was still hiding parts of myself.

I am angry about a lot of things and worry now by typing this that I have opened Pandora's Box. I am angry that Damien took my innocence from me. I am angry that I didn't have anything to save for my future husband. I am angry that he isn't sorry for what he stole from me. I am angry that my mother chose to protect my brother rather than help me. I am angry that it has made me feel small and unworthy. I am angry that I have carried the hurt into my relationships. I am angry that the pain makes me question my ability as a woman, a wife, and a parent.

I am angry that no one saw the signs and helped me. I am angry that my mother didn't protect me. I am angry that my mother never put my needs above her own. I am angry that my life always feels like a battle. I am angry that I was put in a position to hide part of myself from my father. I am angry that when he did find out, he wasn't angry at my mother. I am angry that I feel like I can't remember the good times for shutting out the bad ones. I am angry that I didn't learn to create healthy boundaries for myself. I am angry that I have spent my whole life waiting to be normal. I am angry that I have carried my own wounds into parenting my children. I am angry that I learned more about being a mother from what my mother didn't do or be for me. I am angry that I am always looking for people's unspoken intentions. I am angry that I learned that my body felt like a bargaining tool. I am angry that I have always felt like people would disappoint me, and I just waited for it to happen. I am angry that I always feel lost. I am angry that I always feel a degree of anger. I am angry that I feel alone.

This is a very difficult thing for me to talk about. I always had this idea that if I kept all those feelings of anger and betrayal shoved into a closet that I would feel more safe, more at peace. I remember feeling like my therapist wanted to laugh at how certain I was that it was all in the closet. The idea that just because I said that it was true, somehow made it so. I logically knew that I was angry. I logically knew that it affected me and all my relationships, but as long as it went unacknowledged, I didn't have to address it. I never addressed it in therapy, because it was a subject that scared me.

I remember during the more intense therapy sessions, we tried everything to get me to go there, and I would always stop myself. I refused to let myself feel anything very deep. I lost so much time and wasted so much energy refusing to go beyond the surface. Guess what? I have been typing on and off for months, allowing myself to feel as deeply as I needed to in order to write this book, and no one has been hurt from flying pieces of Pam exploding from the closet of untouched emotions. I am the one giving power to all those feelings in that closet. I make them so much bigger than they are. Just saying I wasn't angry didn't make it so. I have obviously been angry the entire time, just choosing not to acknowledge it. My power has always been in my reaction to the anger. I give all those feelings life, or as much life as I choose to give it. I am not powerless to my anger, and I have never been powerless to it. It is the one thing that gives me power. Damien, my mom, other people who hurt and disappointed me, cannot add to, take away, or control my reaction or how I feel.

Anger feeds a lot of things in our lives. It can be a tool or a detriment and I can see so many examples of how I used it for both. Anger drove me and was fuel for me to determine who I wanted to be. It drove me to want to be a good woman, a good wife, a good mother, a good person. It drove me to not let the things that had happened to me be an excuse for letting myself down. It gave me strength when I felt like I had been wronged, to want a better outcome. I have also used it as an excuse to stay away from dealing with anything that scared me. It made me hide parts of me from the people I loved out of fear. It kept me from experiencing life, and making myself just a passenger at a lot of crucial junctures in my life. It gave me an excuse to keep my expectations low, both of myself and others. I gave it the power to hide in that closet.

    I want you to know that of all the things I have typed, this chapter about anger was probably the easiest. I have wasted too much time, and certainly too much energy, being scared of something that had no power over me. At any other time in my life I would have wasted more time and energy beating myself up over the lost time and energy. I find it funny today that I was so scared of letting myself think about all the things I am angry about. That was about as useless as worrying about whether the sky will still be blue in the morning when I wake up. Oh wait, I think I did tell my therapist that I even worried about that.

Sense of Loss

Experiencing a sense of loss seems like an odd feeling to associate with sexual or emotional abuse, but it is something that always feels close to the surface when I allow myself to think about my life. I feel the loss of my childhood, my innocence. Since I can't remember a time before the abuse started, I mourned my lost childhood. There isn't a time that I can remember not being scared as a child. I didn't get to go through the periods of just being scared of the dark, or of clowns. I was worried about things that I shouldn't even know about. I was scared of being pregnant, I was scared of bleeding through my panties because of the damage the night before. I was scared of being inappropriate because I forgot to switch roles. I was scared of everyone knowing that I was damaged goods. I have always felt too old for my life.

In looking back at my life, I am most sad about how much time I wasted. I always felt like a passenger in my life, rather than the driver. I was so wrapped up in controlling myself and worrying about appearing normal that I rarely let myself experience things and I've missed the joy of things. I mourn my childhood and teen years because of it.

I mourn having innocence to give away on my own terms. I mourn the loss of innocence that prevented me from believing a boy or man could enjoy my company without any sexual expectation. I started dating at the age of fourteen. It never occurred to me to not give in to someone. I had spent my entire life in church and professing my faith but I was different than those people. I was so damaged that I never expected a normal relationship or interaction with people. I pretended to be normal, as best I could, but the pretending damaged me more than the abuse.

    I feel a sense of loss for who I could have been. If I had been born into a different life, would I have felt whole, less dirty? Who knows if that is true or even rational, but I do feel an overwhelming sense of loss for who I could have been and what I could have done and contributed? I am not saying I don't love myself or who I have become. I mourn that little girl before all the shame and anger became her way of life for so long. This emotion reminds me of another conversation with my therapist. At one of our sessions, she asked me to bring pictures of me as a child from as early as I could find through my early adulthood. I remember going through those pictures and looking at them with her and having a long conversation about my eyes. You can tell in those pictures so much about my emotional state by my eyes. My eyes have always been like mood rings, changing intensity and even color with my state of mind.

Who Did You See?

Although my Dad and I always joked about it, I never truly looked at those pictures with that in mind. You can see distinct sadness in some of the pictures we looked at that day. I brought boxes and boxes of pictures from my mother's house when I started typing this book. I find myself always looking at my eyes now and wondering about the girl in the pictures. The eyes truly are a window to the soul, and in most of my childhood pictures, I see a child in crisis, and in others, I see sadness. However, there is always a flicker of love and hope, too, if you look closely enough.

I wonder now if this overwhelming sense of loss is why I felt such anger when my brother, sister, and father died. The mourning that accompanies death felt way too familiar to me. It brought up an exhaustion that had been simmering beneath the surface for a very long time. Exhaustion from mourning my innocence, my childhood, thinking about who I could have been. It brought up the anger that had always been there.

Pamela Chastain

Momma – The Early Years

The pain associated with the relationship between my mother and me is the one I struggle with the most. It brings me a deep pain and rawness that the other parts of my story do not. I have always felt the sting of not being wanted by her. I will admit that it is difficult for me to separate what is coming directly from her from what I am carrying myself; but warranted or not, that is simply how I have always felt. From the beginning, she openly let Alecia fill her role with me. She laughs to this day about how Alecia just took over and took care of me. She has also openly admitted on numerous occasions that she didn't want another child. I have no memories of good times that we shared bonding over the things that I do with my own children. The fondest memory I have of a bonding moment as a child is sitting next to her in church and picking off the clear nail polish on her long thumbnail.

I don't remember any soft and lingering moments with her, just with my sister. I always felt like a bother to her. She didn't like my need to ask questions. She didn't like my need to debate anything, and she certainly didn't seem to like that I was the apple of my father's eye. My mother was needy. She would soak up every ounce of pity in a room like a sponge. She lived for it, and I have never experienced anything else like it in my life. I understand now that she was depressed and struggling with her issues with alcohol, but as a child all I knew was that she didn't want to be bothered with me.

My mother lives in her own world that I will never fully understand. She manipulated the people around her to get her out of a self-created drama. Whenever something was not going her way, she played sick. She would have fainting spells or throw herself down the stairs. The problem is that she is a terrible actress and we all knew what she was doing. I will never know if my father knew, we never spoke about it directly, but she was always leaning up and looking around to see if anyone was about to find her when she "fainted" – not very convincing. Or even worse, she would leave the house threatening to run away and never come back because we were going to tell my father what was going on. She would leave, crying hysterically, with a huff that "he would leave her anyway" so she should just leave since we didn't care what happened to her. It was sheer manipulation that we fell for every time. When she wasn't pretending to be either sick or hurt, she was lying around feeling sorry for herself. I know now, she was struggling with an alcohol addiction, but as a child, I didn't understand that. All I knew was that Mom had no interest in me because she bluntly told me, often. In public, she put on a completely different persona of an interested and vested parent.

She made me feel invisible and a bother to her. I felt discarded by her. Leading up to my eighth-grade year, my situation with my brother and mother was coming to a head. My brother was getting married and my mother was insisting that we must be in his wedding. I had put up with a lot, I had always wondered where the line was that I wouldn't cross. Well this was it. I confronted my mother, and she did exactly what I was expecting. She downplayed everything that I told her had happened—again. When I fought back, she walked out with a dramatic flair, thanking me for being so selfish and for ruining her life. I remember something snapping in me that time. I didn't start to cry, I didn't grab her arm. I didn't run after her, I let her go. Watching her walk away, something broke in me that day that still doesn't feel healed. Sadly, I think it broke for my mother as well.

At some point she came home, and I couldn't tell you when we began to speak again. I can tell you that she didn't hear me at all, because the next blowup was still about Damien and his wedding. Damien wanted me to go with him to pick out his wife's wedding present. Yep, you guessed it. Mom demanded I go with him. Damien sat at the table gloating while she informed me that I would go with him because we needed to "make up" before the wedding. I remember the look on his face; it was the same face he made standing at Walmart years later almost laughing at the way my voice quivered. I was forced to go with him. I begrudgingly got into the car and we drove to the mall. The moment we arrived, I opened the car door and knew I couldn't go inside with him. I shut the door and started walking home. I just couldn't do it. The idea of walking into the store and being part of this farce and manipulation was enough. Damien caught up with me in the car and laughed at me, yelled at me, pleaded with me, even. I eventually got back in the car and he took me home. That was the last time I was ever alone with him, and the first time I stood up for myself. It felt freeing, I began to feel my wings a little that day. They were still weak, but at least I had an idea they were there.

  I could type more stories, but honestly, they are just more of the same. This is what the relationship between my mother and I looked like. I knew my mother's story, and I knew the pain and heartache that she carried with her into our lives and her parenting. My father, brother, and sister all gave her a pass for it. They all seemed oblivious to her shortcomings and ignored her abusive behavior. It was just expected that I should suck it up and move on. Somehow, I couldn't do it. Maybe it was because they felt the warmth of her love which I don't remember experiencing, or maybe she was right, I was selfish and only would think of myself. That is something I have struggled with my whole life. What I do know, is that who I am as a mother, a wife, and a woman is a reflection of who she was not.

    The Christmas before my dad passed away we spent in the ICU. His cancer was back for the third and final time and we knew this was the beginning of the end. It was metastatic and we would not be spending Christmas at home this year. I bought a gold cross for my father to give to my Mom in the hospital for Christmas, and I remember the love in his eyes when he gave it to her. At those moments, I felt so empty wishing that I could summon up feelings for her like they shared. That night a nurse my mother knew was taking care of him in the ICU. I remember sitting there, already struggling with so much and my mom introducing me to her. My mother talked about losing my brother and sister and said, "You know I never wanted another child and I cried every day for the first several years after Pam was born, but God knows what He is doing. If I hadn't had her, who would be left here to take care of us since Alecia and John are gone?" That sums up our relationship, that sums up my purpose in my mother's eyes and will always be what I think of when she looks at me.

    I wish I could say that it was something said without thought, or because she was exhausted and scared. It was the first time I believe my mother told the truth to anyone, including me, about how she felt about me. It confirmed how I saw my mother for all those years. I always believed not only that I was unwanted by her, but that we were just all there to fulfill something she wanted or needed. I wasn't valued for who I was or could be, I was valued by whatever purpose I fulfilled for her. She is one of the most selfish people I have ever known.

The Tables Will Turn

Mom insisted for years that she had no contact with Damien. She wanted me to believe that she was making things right after my father learned what happened and that she was cutting off contact with him. But I never believed it. I wanted to believe it, but I had this nagging feeling that she wasn't being honest. The crippling reality I learned from the Walmart reunion with Damien was that she had indeed lied to me again and to my father. Come to find out, she had been in communication with him and his family, taking presents to them, and they were completely aware of the details of all our lives. I never asked her to cut off contact with Damien. I never want to be in a position to ask anything of her and risk more disappointment. She made this grand gesture to make an attempt to make amends for covering up the truth. That was much more important to my sister and brother than it was to me because I had no true relationship with her beyond a surface version for my father. That information just didn't rip off a band aid on an old wound, it was proof that not only was she incapable of being honest to me, but that she would always choose Damien, given the opportunity.

I never told my father, just like all the other times she hurt me. I never confronted her about it until many years later and I did what I had always done. I hurt in silence. I took in the pain, the betrayal, the feeling that I couldn't rely on anyone else and put it into a closet. Years would pass, John would be taken, Daddy would go back into his health battle, and I would struggle to keep myself together, and not much would change with this relationship with my mother.

When my father was sick and in his last days at home, my mother's alcoholism was in full swing. I was spending every minute that I could with him, working full-time, dealing with the drama in my marriage and raising children. One day while at work, my mom called crying hysterically saying that he had fallen and she couldn't get him off the floor. I could tell from her voice that she was drinking, she was in full cover mode, in what I also always refer to as "full-on Mom mode." She knows that if she is pitiful, incapable, and out of control, she usually gets away with whatever she had done because we get so busy cleaning up her mess that we don't have the energy to address her. I didn't care at the time, I just wanted to get to him. When I got to him, he was lying on the floor covered in urine and sitting in his own feces crying. He was embarrassed and, sadly, more worried about Mom than himself. Mom, well she shut herself in her room wailing as soon as I got there. I got him up, cleaned him up, made him some dinner and turned the TV as loud as we could stand it to drown out her attention-seeking from her bedroom. The louder she wailed, the angrier I got. She had clearly had too much to drink and my father deserved better. I knew then that we needed help and called in hospice care against both of their wishes. I don't know how I would have gotten through that time without them. They cared not only for Dad, but for me. They prepared me in the ways they could for what was happening. They also recognized very quickly the issues with my mom's drinking. I was called more than once threatening they would have to remove him from the home if I either couldn't be there or if she couldn't control herself. My father deteriorated quickly, and Mom continued to drink heavily. It is one more time that my mother showed her weakness to me. He was the single person in her life that loved her unconditionally. He adored her, faults and all, and she was once again putting herself first.

    Now, I know all of you are asking me why I couldn't see her side. She is losing her one true love, and shouldn't I give her grace? Yes, I should have. I should have been more tolerant, and I should have been more kind to her. Sometimes, I spend a lot of energy wishing I could have been. It does haunt me—I want to be a better person than that. All I can tell you is that I didn't have an ounce more of compassion in me. That rope had been stretched, and stretched, and stretched. I think back to that time in my life and I truly do not know how I survived it. I pushed all that anger toward my mother into a closet. I knew if it ever got out, Lord help her.

This pain from the relationship with my mother has been the single biggest obstacle of my life and I find myself struggling with it still today. When Dad passed away, I took mom in just like I promised him. I moved her in with me until two years ago when Alan and I married. I would love to tell you a story of healing, but I don't have one yet. I have found some peace with the situation and have quit letting it make me doubt if I am worthy of love, or worse, if I will become her, but it is a constant struggle. Not only that, but the irony is not lost on me that the one person who I believe is most responsible for the damage to my soul is the only family I have left.

Mom and I have had some difficult times over the last several years. She was accustomed to my dad enabling her behavior, but I was not going to do that. I had certainly been guilty of the same in the past, or maybe more so, just ignoring it. Now, she was under the same roof as the children I loved and promised to protect. I would never allow that behavior, or would I? Would I be strong enough to confront her with a mirror? If I did, would I be brave enough to look in it myself?

    The agreement between my mother and me when she moved in was that she could not drink—period. She was able to keep the agreement for a while, but even though she lived with us, she wanted nothing to do with us in general. She isn't that doting grandma. She doesn't want to play or hang out or do much of anything with the kids. She wants to sit in the dark in her room and be left alone. You see, she doesn't want to be here. She has never wanted to be here. She has spent the entire time I have known her waiting to die, and often making up illnesses so we thought she would. She told me when I was a senior in high school that she had brain cancer.

    Whenever Mom would begin to drink, she would have to leave. She would go somewhere, get sobered up and come back home, until the final blowup several years ago. All her hatred, anger, and resentment toward me had been building for a very long time and she finally had enough to drink that it all came pouring out. I was in my room working on my computer and she stumbled in and in an almost incoherent drunken state began to berate me for every perceived slight my kids and I had ever dealt her.

Who Did You See?

My mother is a mean drunk. Luckily for her, she never remembers it but always manages to hit wounds deep enough that you are never able to forget it. I still have the video and after listening to it again, my stomach feels just as sick. Everything that has happened since the day I was born to her is my fault, somehow. She thinks I am a terrible wife, she thinks I am a horrible mother, but most of all I am a terrible daughter. She left that night drunk in her car with a bag packed. I was so angry, so tired, and so incredibly relieved she was gone. The kids were at their father's house and Alan was at drill in Knoxville, so she had me all to herself. I should not have not let her go in her state; I should not have kept wine in the house for me; and I should not have let her continue to stay with me knowing this blowup was coming.

One of the things she said to me was that if my father knew what a whore I was that he wouldn't have loved me. She knew where to hit me; she always did. It just didn't carry the weight that it would have at another point in my life. It actually made me sad for her. She had been waiting a very long time to say that to me, and I had taken one more thing from her, apparently. I took her ability to hurt me away. She didn't have that power over me anymore. I'm not sure at what point that changed; I don't think it was a single thing or a single event. I had been quietly getting stronger, learning to shed a little at a time of the hurt that I had been carrying on my shoulders and hiding in my heart. Everything from an emotional strength standpoint changed for me that day. This could have been one of the most painful moments of my life. She was bringing to life every last fear of what I believed she thought about me, and I didn't wither in defeat! It was a gift. It proved to me that I had the power that I allowed myself to have in this relationship. Hearing it out loud wasn't any more painful than knowing she harbored those feelings.

Our relationship completely changed that day, even if she didn't realize it. There was not this closet trying to burst open with all these unspoken things. She had said all she could, and I was not only standing but leaning into it. I was not "stuck with her," I didn't have to keep her under my roof to keep my promise to my father. I didn't have to be a martyr to show that I was stronger than her, stronger than Damien. I never had to do that, I chose to do that all those years. All I had to do was choose something different. Power is found in the small moments in your life. Power is found when you least expect it, and in the things which show you that you always had it, not that you found it.

I found Mom a roommate and moved her into an apartment close to us. I can tell her I love her. I can grab her what she needs from the store, and I can call on her for help with the kids when they need a ride to something around town that I can't get them to. We love each other; we just don't like each other. You know what—it's okay. I can't change her. I can't make her want to come for dinner, although she is invited. I can't make her want to enjoy her grandkids, although they are amazing. I can't make her want to live and quit hoping she'll die, although her health is starting to fail her. I can't make her not take another drink, but I can ensure that if she does, it doesn't hold any power to hurt me or the kids. We may not ever have the relationship that most people would strive for. I may never have the apologies that I believe I am due. We have said all the things we were scared to say to each other now, and we both lived through it. There is joy and healing in peace, and that we do have.

The Cycle of Abuse

The conversation about the cycle of abuse is not a surface conversation; it takes self-reflection which, before now, has been something I would not allow myself to do. I was always irritated with my brother John because he was so outwardly self-abusive. I had a very pious opinion of how I dealt with the abuse, before now.

Stopping the cycle of abuse begins with recognizing how you abuse yourself and the people around you. I was abusing myself. I believe now that I was abusing the people around me. It might have looked different than the way Damien and my mother abused me, but it was still there. I perpetuated it in my life just like other victims, and I had nothing to feel pious about at all. Holding the mirror up to my relationships required that I look just as deeply within myself and I have been much more destructive than John was, I was just better at hiding it. By internalizing all that pain and not sharing it, stress and self-destruction became my way of life.

For example, I fell into one relationship after another with the exact same type of person. When I realized what I had chosen, I ran. I ran as fast and as hard as I could. When I did choose to stay with someone, each had the exact same narcissistic personality. It only took me 46 years to recognize it. Better late than never. From my vantage point now, I can look back and see so clearly my patterns and mistakes. Some of the things I did make me sick to my stomach, and I am too embarrassed to write about them. I thought about leaving this out, but I really do want to be honest, and a big part of my story is how I perpetuated abuse on myself and hid it so greatly from everyone but my sister Alecia. Sometimes now I wonder if I made a game out of trying to shock her. I think I subconsciously believed I would eventually do something that she couldn't forgive. I was wrong. She never excused my behavior, but she loved me in spite of it. I wish I had followed her example. She wanted to rise above what happened and still have self-respect. I just pretended to have self-respect. As long as people believed the facade, it was fine by me.

    I was fourteen when I had my first real boyfriend. When we met it never occurred to me not to have sex with him. I tried very hard to convince myself that I was in love with him, but honestly, I loved the idea that he was completely unconnected to my life. Since I was only 14 and couldn't drive, and he lived an hour away, I could portray myself however I wanted to. We dated for a while, then broke up and reconnected my senior year in high school. Between those years, I would describe my love life as an absolute train wreck. I spent a lot of time with older men. There just isn't a polite way to say I was an opportunist. I spent time with people who I thought would benefit me in some way. I started working at offices at the age of sixteen and would find myself in what I believed were relationships that I could control. I already felt dirty and broken, so what did it matter if I traded my body? It really didn't feel like mine anyway. The oddest part of looking at this now is that my entire life, I have been one of the most judgmental people I know. I wanted to hold everyone accountable but myself.

In the midst of selling myself out, I went to church every time the doors were open with my dad. We didn't just show up on Sunday morning; we participated in everything going on in our church. I spent most summers doing backyard Bible Clubs and visiting and professing my faith, while perpetuating this second life. This need to lead a double life, each in stark contrast, became my escape in some ways. All the while, I was judging everyone else around me. At our church, the husband of one of our youth leaders struck a familiar chord with me. I never trusted him. His looks lingered too long up and down my body, his innuendos put a sick feeling in the pit of my stomach. I made it my purpose to prove what I knew him to be, a predator hiding behind his Christianity and position. I knew the signs; I knew he was grooming me. I had sex with him, and after I told him that if he didn't take his wife and leave our church immediately, I would make sure everyone knew what he was. It never occurred to me what I was giving up for this need to prove that he was a pig. It never occurred to me to hurt for his wife. I didn't like people hiding behind something they were not, although it was exactly how I was living my own life.

I wish that was the only time I used my body to prove a point or to get what I wanted. That is how I lived my life for years. I spent years looking for the type of man who only wanted the one thing I would so freely give. I traded my body for trips out of town, new clothing, or car payments. However, I wouldn't give my heart away. My heart was never involved in these transactions. I held onto the belief that this was what I deserved. The further I sank into that life, the more it proved to me that I was broken and that I was only good for one thing in a relationship. Sex with no intimacy. I let my choices define who I believed myself to be. I know I wanted different but could never lift that mask. If someone tried to peek under that mask, I ran. I ran as fast and as hard as I could.

During my senior year in high school, my first boyfriend and I reunited. I continued to see other men even after he asked me to marry him. I knew all along that he was only with me to thumb his nose at his parents. His family saw me for what I saw myself—a girl from the other side of town who didn't come from much and didn't have much to offer their son. I couldn't blame them, and I couldn't blame him. I understood the need to prove something to a parent. Brad and I never made it past graduation; in fact, he didn't show up to mine. He was drunk on the right side of town at a party. After breaking off that engagement, I sank deeper into the belief that I was unworthy of love.

Along Came Prince Charming - The First One

So, of all the stories in this book, this one will probably make you shake your head. For someone who was looking for love and acceptance, finding it would have been a gift, right? For those of you reading this book who knew my brother John, you will also truly appreciate this story. When I was 18, I worked full-time for a company across town. My brother, however, pursued his love for alcohol most days when he wasn't working. One of those days he was hanging out at Jack Daniel's Saloon and was striking up conversations with strangers. I could say that was unusual, but that would be a lie. He was hanging out at the bar, apparently listening to other people's conversations, and heard something that caught his attention. Sean and his father were in town from Toronto and staying at the Opryland Hotel, and they loved to bet on just about anything. They had a bet going on the Super Bowl and if Sean lost, he had to find the prettiest girl in Nashville to go to dinner with him. John listened and planned on how he could benefit and then my brother offered me up like a seasoned pimp! Can you imagine sitting at work and getting a call from your half-lit brother telling you if you had plans for the night to cancel them because he was setting you up with someone from Canada he met in a bar to win some bet? Most people, most normal people, would have hung up the phone and hit him in the face the next time we were together. Nope, I grabbed my purse and thought this would at least be good for a story. Again, I had no single thought for my personal safety or what might happen to me; I just went along for the ride.

Apparently, the story goes something like this. John overheard his conversation with the bartender and John said, "Hey, my sister will go out with you." Now, I can look at this two different ways. One, my brother heard the words "prettiest girl in Nashville" and thought of me (win), or two, there was a bet and he wanted the money at whatever expense to his sister (not so much a win). Regardless, I drove across town and went to meet who would end up being my first husband. I walked into the bar with my obligatory shit-kickers on and ready to see what John was making such a fuss about. Sitting at the bar with my brother was a very handsome man laughing like they had been friends for years. Sean has a sparkle in his eye that is hard to describe. Sean does everything 100% all the time, which can be good or bad depending on where his intentions are, but he just can't seem to do anything halfway. That can be very intoxicating when you are looking to fill a void.

It has been a long time since that night, but I remember feeling like I had known him my whole

Who Did You See?

life. He made me laugh, he made me feel beautiful and wanted, and he made me feel like no one else mattered but me. While he was in town, we spent every moment together we could and I expected that would be it, no matter what he said. People never kept their word and I assumed he had gotten what he wanted, so I would never hear from him again, I was wrong. Along came beautiful roses and a plane ticket to Toronto to see him. Sean completely swept me off my feet. We were two kids, playing adult and carrying our own baggage and looking for that other person to make us feel complete. It was intoxicating. I felt free there, I felt like the pain and baggage from home was swept away. Could I have a new life there? Could I leave all the turmoil behind and start over? I wanted to, but another part of me wanted to run away from him.

Sean and I started making plans quickly for me to move to Canada with him, but once again my family stood in my way. My "Southern Baptist family" couldn't live with the idea of me moving if we weren't married, so Sean popped the question. We quickly put the wedding together and put in motion the plan for running away from my life in Nashville. The idea of leaving my sister, my dad, and my brother was crushing, but it didn't trump the idea of getting away from all the difficult memories and painful relationships.

Pamela Chastain

We got married December 26, 1990. We spent the night in Nashville but left the following morning on our adventure back to Canada to start our new life together. The very first day was an adventure because we were driving in an ice storm. I remember being certain we would die, but we made it! I remember feeling more and more free the farther we drove from Tennessee. Everything about our new life felt like a field trip to me. Sean adored me, I woke up every day wondering what fun new thing would happen to us. I don't remember every detail of our lives. Maybe a lot of it is because I don't want to think about how things would have been if I had made different decisions.

When we arrived in Orillia, Ontario, Sean had his own business and we were living in a house that his father owned. One day, things started to unravel, and his father wanted us to move out. We were off on another adventure. His mother lived in Prince George, British Columbia, and was going to help us establish ourselves there. I want you to think about two young kids having no jobs and nothing but what we fit into my car and no sure plans for the future, driving across Canada during the winter. We weren't stressed out, we weren't scared—or at least I wasn't. I was exhilarated. None of this felt like anything close to the stress that I lived with every day at home; however, I began to feel a deep nagging at my heart. I missed my family in a way that I didn't expect. I think this was where my life took another drastic turn emotionally.

    I had always lived in almost a fight-or-flight emotional state. I got up every day just trying to survive the myriad of situations at home. I constantly felt like I might just die from the stress, to be honest. When I first left, I felt free. It felt so good to be testing my own wings. I loved this new feeling of freedom. Then, as I began to feel more safe and less like I was on a field trip, I remember a change that crept in a little deeper into my soul every day. First, I think it was just an overwhelming sadness that I missed Alecia, John, and Daddy. Then, it changed. It became this overwhelming fear that I was so far away, and I didn't really know any of these people. I began to second-guess everything they told me, and everything that I believed was true before.

    Sean found a job working at a shoe store, but we were back where he grew up. These were his friends. Slowly it began to feel like I was fading away again. At home, I always had this overwhelming feeling like I was just part of the backdrop of whatever was going on. I never felt like I was a real part of decisions; I just had to walk through everyone else's life. My new life began to feel the same way. I felt myself begin to withdraw.

The pain and worry of being away from Alecia was always there, but now it began to take over my thoughts all the time. This was a slippery slope that felt very familiar. It starts with feelings of loneliness, then come the feelings of self-doubt and unworthiness, then comes the need to run, to run before getting hurt again.

I had put myself in a situation that gave me absolutely no control. I had moved half a world away, couldn't work there, had no family or friends of my own, and I felt Sean pulling away. I had convinced myself that the falling out with his dad was my fault and I knew Sean was not happy working at a shoe store. Our life didn't look like either of us thought it would, and I was certain that it was my fault. I had begun a friendship with a girl I met there, and in looking back I am not certain she was a great fan of Sean. She always arrived with a story of who Sean was talking to that day, or what girl was flirting with him. When Sean walked in the door, I always seemed to forget completely all my doubts and fears. He looked at me every time he walked in like the first time he saw me. We were playing house, learning to cook together, and dragging our mattress onto the living room floor to play "Naked Mario." However, the minute he left, I would fall deeper and deeper into depression and self-doubt. Two major things started me on a rapid downward path; my sister decided Daddy should know what had happened to us, and Sean was being offered another job. And this job was a few hours away, which meant another move.

I remember having a very long conversation on the phone with Alecia about her decision to tell Daddy. Damien, being invited to our wedding against my wishes, and Mom encouraging him to be at every holiday had become too much for her to bear. It was different for her now that she had children. For years, Alecia had been the "compliant" of the three of us. She never brought up what happened, never seemed angry or even affected by what happened. I knew she was. I knew how it tormented her dreams and kept her from allowing her children to be alone with anyone, not even in the room together alone. She was just better at hiding it with everyone but with me, which brings up another difficult thing for me to explain.

Alecia and I were closer than I can explain, or even justify. Whether it was because I was her birthday present, whether it was because of our shared abuse, or maybe just because she loved in such an unselfish and amazing way, we were always more than just sisters. Nothing felt real until we shared it with each other. We could finish each other's sentences, and I never felt right when I was away from her. For the first time in her life she began to understand my anger with Mom. She wanted Daddy to understand why things had become so strained. She had finally become tired of letting Mom play the victim while we suffered. She was also terrified of the aftermath, but she was always the braver one. That isn't a statement to get compliments; it is the truth.

I didn't know until then that she told Daddy the first time Damien touched her. I don't know all the details, but I do know that when she told him, he beat Damien. From Alecia's version, she was scared he was going to kill him. She never told Daddy anything else after that. She knew that I had told Mom, she knew that she had told Daddy, and I don't think Alecia would have ever said anything had it all not come to a head at my wedding. Alecia felt like I had run away because of what happened. Now it seemed to be like a wound that wouldn't heal for her and she refused to live that way. I remember being so confused about how to feel. I wanted him to know, but I never wanted anything to change the way he felt about me. Would he feel betrayed and angry? Would he kill Damien? Would Daddy go to jail? Would he divorce Mom for hiding it all these years?

The questions and fear began to run like a loop through my brain. I couldn't think about Sean and our future. I couldn't think about the move he needed me to make. I couldn't think about anything but my sister facing telling Daddy what happened to us on her own. I began to be suspicious of everything Sean said and did. I wanted to believe he wasn't who I thought he was. I knew I had to go home, and I couldn't bear the thought of leaving someone who loved me. I convinced myself that he didn't. I convinced myself that he was seeing someone else. I convinced myself that the rift with his dad was my fault. Most of all I convinced myself that he would be better off without me.

I knew my sister would never let me leave him and come home unless she believed that he had hurt me. She would never have let me sacrifice anything for her unless she believed I had to come home. This would be another moment that I will always wish I could go back to. I called her and told her that he had cheated on me. I told her I had to come home, and that I needed her to wait to tell Daddy because I couldn't handle any more right then. Once the wheels were set into motion, there was no turning back. I was leaving the one person who had willingly chosen to love me, the screwed-up mess that I was. I would never know what it felt like to grow old with someone who loved me. I would never have a chance to see what life would be like away from the pain and memories at home. I was lying and hurting the one person who had finally put me first. I began to believe that I was no better than my mother, a belief that I held onto for decades. I was running back to all the memories and pain that I had escaped, by my own choice. It absolutely proved to me that I would never be able to find love or feel whole.

Coming Home

If there is a story in this book that is a reflection of my life, it is this one. I left Sean, not knowing truly why or what he had done. I left him to pick up his own pieces and I ran home to the place where I knew what to expect—heartache and disappointment. Now this is where the story gets even more complicated. I packed my car with just what I thought I could cross the border with, my family wired me $200, and I had to drive to Sacramento to stay with my grandmother. I had no idea what I was in for.

It is hard to imagine for kids today what it would be like to make a trip like that. No GPS, no cell phone, no help if I got lost or hurt. I left completely broken. I knew I was hurting him. I knew I was leaving the opportunity to be loved and I knew I was going home to face telling my dad what happened. As I write this, my stomach hurts as well as my heart. My car was a joke. It was already a joke here in Nashville, but it was more of a joke facing Canadian snow. My first stop was for a map and a highlighter. I had to buy more than one map, actually more than two. I cried so hard trying to map out my path that I ripped the first two. Sometimes I wonder if I didn't believe I would make it and that this was my attempt at hoping that God would finally take mercy on me.

    The first 24 hours were relatively uneventful, other than stopping frequently because I was overwhelmed. I cried so much during those first 24 hours that I still do not understand how I was able to see the road. I would drive for a few hours and then pull over to the side of the road and cry. I wept until I was spent, got myself together, and got back on the road. Oddly enough, I remember nothing of the scenery. I drove through some of the most beautiful parts of British Columbia, but I do not remember a single mental snapshot of the beauty that I saw. As I was driving into the second night, I remember feeling an exhaustion that I cannot explain. I had been living on adrenaline for so long that I felt like I could not go any farther. I saw a blinking motel sign appear out of nowhere. When I pulled into the courtyard, I saw rooms that opened to the driveway and there was a large group of loud, drunk people congregating in the parking lot. I thought about turning around, but my body said no. I checked in and dashed into my room like my life depended on it (and now I am sure it did). As I ran, loud drunk comments, yelling and whistling followed me along with what sounded like running. I have never run so quickly in my life. I ended up in my room with nothing but my keys and purse. I angled the chair under the door handle and crawled on the filthy bed and wept. I wept for much more than just being scared.

I felt such overwhelming loss—loss of so much more than I understood at the moment. I can see that night now, and I know that it was more mourning than fear. I was mourning the loss of so many things, including my dream that I could escape the past by running away from Nashville and my family. I was so very young but felt so very old. I had spent my life running. I was always running from the abuse while I was growing up, pretending to be what everyone else wanted. I ran away from that to what I thought would make me feel safe. Now, I was running from that! I was sitting in a room alone and scared half to death, knowing that if I made it through the night, the fear of facing how my dad would look at me when he found out the truth was waiting for me.

I picked up the phone to call the front desk and the phone didn't work. I sat on the bed literally frozen because someone kept trying the door handle. I have never been so scared in my life. I had left someone who loved me, who would have protected and loved me, to go home and face my worst fears at home—and now, it seemed I would just die somewhere in the mountains and no one would ever know what happened to me. I sat there as still as I could until the sounds outside died down, and I ran to my car as quickly as I had run to what I believed was the safety of a room where I could sleep. I jumped in my car, sped off, and got back on the road. Most of you who don't know me, and my bad luck would think this would be where the story got a little better. Nope—my night was just beginning to go down the tubes.

I was angry—angrier than I had been in a very long time. I banged the steering wheel with my hands, cursing and yelling at God. Why in the world did God hate me this much? Why in the world could I never catch a break? Why was He tormenting me? As I circled the rim of deep depression, bang—my driver's side window slid completely down into my door. With a loud snap it had disappeared. Let's not forget that it was the middle of the night. And don't forget that I was in the middle of the mountains, in the freezing cold! As I pulled over at the next exit, and got out of my car to figure out what was going on, guess what? It began to snow.

This is one of those moments in my life that I think I may have had a mini breakdown. I sat on the ground, in the snow, in the middle of nowhere, and began to laugh. I laughed so hard I wet my pants. I had absolutely no idea what to do. After realizing that my hands and face were getting numb, I got up, popped the trunk of my car and

Who Did You See?

proceeded to put every article of clothing on that I could wear and still drive – through the mountains, in the snow with my window down. I got back on the road, driving pretty slowly with five layers of clothing, my gloves, earmuffs and a stocking cap driving through the mountains in the middle of the night in the snow. It didn't matter to me how slowly I was moving, just that I kept moving. It was actually a battle for me at that point, and I wouldn't lose!

Well, that was my belief until my face was so cold and chapped that I felt it cracking. I pulled over again at a McDonalds to warm up and decided to see if I could pull up the window. I grabbed a huge pile of napkins and I managed to pull the window up and I stuffed the napkins between the rubber and the glass. Since the snow had stopped, I thought it might last a while. I got back on the road, but I kept all my clothing close just in case. I drove for a few hours and about the time I began to let my guard down, it started snowing again. The napkins got wet and with a familiar noise the window slipped back into the door.

The sun started to come up and I had lived through what was one of the loneliest, scariest, yet monumental, nights of my life. I stopped for gas at the next city and next door was an auto repair place. I parked, shoved more napkins in my window, and slept. I remember an older gentleman knocking on the window, the window falling down again, and his laughter as he said, "Well, I guess I know why you are parked in front of my shop." As I sat with him over coffee in his little warm shop, telling him the story of what had happened, I will always remember what he said to me. Art lovingly smiled at me, he patted my hand and said, "Well little miss, God always brings us to the people we need and who need us the most at just the right time."

He explained that he could order the parts to fix my window for me, but he wouldn't have them for a few days. He said he would be happy to take me home to his wife so she could love on me for those few days. As I sat there with him, he explained that his daughter had died in an accident several years before. She was on the way back from a ski trip with her friends and had fallen asleep at the wheel. I wish I had taken him up on the offer. I think about that woman I never took the time to meet a lot, and I pray for her and for that kind man. That was selfish of me. I appreciated his kindness, and I think that was a moment that God needed me to go be there for that family and I didn't do it. I regret that decision.

I make a conscious effort now to listen to that pull on my heart, even when I don't feel like I have time. Art found a small piece of rubber that he cut to fit against the glass to keep the window from sliding back down. He fed me breakfast at the diner, while I listened to him tell me stories about Tia, who was about my age. I hugged him tightly, I kissed him on the forehead, and I told him that his daughter was a very lucky girl and I am sure that she was with him every single day. That man and his kindness is one of the things that reminds me how much God has kept His hand on my shoulder, even when I felt utterly alone.

The rigged window was working pretty well. It held for a few hours at a time, which made me stop and take a break, which I would not have done otherwise. The rest of the trip to Sacramento was relatively uneventful and I made it safely to my grandmother's house.

This story is such a snapshot of my life as I look back at it now. I have had a difficult life. Not the worst that I know of, certainly not the best, either. I felt like I was in a continuous struggle. It seemed that I went from one difficult situation to another, with very little time to lick my wounds. My life has never been easy. However, my life has ALWAYS been touched in every difficult struggle by the one who saved me from myself and my feelings of despair. God has shown his love to me over and over again with people who show up at just the right time to remind me who I want to be. I want to be like that kind man who knew what to say and who to be to that broken little girl. If I hide my wounds from everyone, if I don't share where I have been, I can't share in those moments like Art did for me. He didn't have to show me his pain; he didn't have to share his stories and his tears. He is a reminder to me that I have never, ever been alone. God has been with me for every single heartbeat, every single moment of laughter, and most importantly, every single moment of despair. He sent so many angels to me when I needed them the most, and I have been loved and treasured by him even when I felt empty and alone.

Coming Home – Scene 2

For those of you who think that Sacramento is a long way from Nashville, you are correct. I still had another adventure ahead. Growing up, I had only spent time with my grandmother once in Nashville. I had never met most of my family in Sacramento, other than when I was 5. I had a whole month to recoup under my grandmother's sweet tender care. I had heard so many stories about this woman from my dad, but honestly, I didn't know her. I didn't know my cousins, and I needed some time to feel ready for the battle brewing at home. My grandmother Elsie had outlived two husbands and was as feisty and sweet as anyone I have ever met. My dad had a very rough childhood. There are several books that he could have written about enduring childhood trauma and learning to be a man on his own.

My dad was the oldest of three boys. He came from nothing. He told me a story once about how they were literally living in a chicken coop while his father was building their house when he was very small. They didn't have any money for food, and he and his brothers found a nearby orchard of fig trees. He told me he ate so many of them that he was sick for days. He couldn't even think about them without feeling ill for the rest of his life. He loved his mother, but he had an odd, unemotional relationship with her. It certainly wasn't the way he loved me, or my own mother. He called her once a week and asked appropriate questions, but there never seemed to be a lot of sadness that they weren't in each other's lives. Grandma came to visit once when I was in elementary school and that was it. I was in Sacramento for a whole month and I wasn't sure what to expect. I was shocked when I first saw her. She looked small and fragile, and her hands would shake a lot. Looking back, I think a lot of it was an emotional response because she was so happy that I was there.

My grandfather was a horrible man. He beat her and he beat his three sons relentlessly. He was a raging alcoholic, and from what I can piece together, he wasn't any nicer when he was sober. My dad, as the oldest of the boys, felt responsible for his family, and as the years went by it got harder and harder for him to deal with such an impossible situation. I don't know much, and the stories that I do know came out of some difficult conversations when he was sick, much later than this visit with my grandmother. My father recalled one of the events that led him to lying about his age and joining the Army. He came home to find his mother unconscious and his brothers hiding in the closet with wounds of their own.

Who Did You See?

He became so angry that he beat his father and managed to wrap a fire poker around his neck. He told me that had he not left, he knew that he would kill him. He knew he had to run to save both of their lives. Sadly, he didn't. Not long after my father left to join the Army, someone locked his father in an abandoned house and set it on fire. My father did not come home to attend the funeral. He was not sorry that he was gone, and he sent most of his paychecks home to his family.

I am not sure I understood what significance this visit held for my grandmother then, but I do now that I have spent the last few months making peace with my past. We spent hours upon hours telling stories to each other, getting to know each other, and even sleeping in the same bed because it made us both feel better.

It was an amazing month. I spent time with all my cousins—I had never met most of them. I got to experience what it was like to have extended family, and I loved it. My cousin had his friend rent a little plane and we flew to Palm Springs. I finally let my guard down and could breathe without feeling the fight-or-flight sensation building in my chest. My grandmother and I would have coffee and donuts and laugh until our stomachs hurt. She went through boxes and boxes of pictures and my dad's earliest paintings and drawings. I felt like I got to know my dad in such a sweet and genuine way. It was amazing, until my time there started to run down. The plan was that John would fly out, spend a few days, and then we would drive home together. After the debacle of getting to my grandmother's house, I was a little gun-shy about the drive across country since I was convinced God must be really, really angry with me about something.

As nervous as I was about facing everything at home, it kept my mind from wandering back to what I had lost in Canada. I was not at all dealing with my broken heart and I pushed it into a closet that held all the other disappointments. I think the hardest part about this one is that I couldn't blame anyone but myself for the hole in my heart. I forced myself not to think about what Sean must have been going through. I convinced myself he was better off without me.

When John stepped off the plane in Sacramento, I ran across the terminal and hugged him so hard we both fell over. He cried and cried, and I remember the guilt I felt for that. He thought Sean had hurt me and he felt responsible for that. A good person, a good sister, would have told him the truth, but I couldn't. I couldn't face any of it. I started this journey home to face what I had run away from and I needed to finish it.

Who Did You See?

John came to Grandma's house and got to bask in her love and tender care for a week. We had always been so starved for family, and I watched John blossom in Grandma's love. He was relaxed, he wasn't drinking, and he laughed and laughed with us like he had not done in a very long time. I had missed him so much. My relationship with John was always different and more difficult than my relationship with Alecia. I loved him—I adored him actually—but things with him were always so "messy." He seemed to wear everything that happened to us across his chest and it had always embarrassed me, because I didn't want anyone to know any of it. I wish I had been more patient and more compassionate with him. I missed more times like the time we had there because of it.

After we had eaten too much, been spoiled too much, and laughed way too much, we set off on the trip home. I was desperately brokenhearted and scared to death, but so happy that I didn't have to make this trip alone. We bought a new map and some highlighters—this couldn't be too bad, right? I pulled over a few miles from Grandma's house and John and I mapped out our route, decided when we would plan to stop and sleep, and I would take the first shift and drive until I couldn't drive anymore. That meant John should sleep, which gave me too much time with my thoughts. As if on cue, my window would fall every few hours. Every time it fell, I felt the same mix of laughter and tears. John was sound asleep, open mouth snoring continuously if we were not stopped for gas or food. He was little to no help at all and I found myself irritated and frustrated. I had lost sight of the fact that I had someone with me and that was the biggest blessing of all. Then, God decided to remind me that I had a lot to be thankful for.

I was driving in the middle of the desert, with no one on the interstate for miles when my car's computer lost its mind. Normally, if the internal check set off something within the computer, everything would shut down (radio, air conditioner, etc), and it would speak what it wanted and then everything would start back up. Well, it decided to run on some crazy continuous loop. It wouldn't shut up! It had caution lights on. Everything on the car was yapping non-stop about the brake pads, my fuel level, the oil change, and the doors being ajar. The worst part, we were in the middle of the desert and the air conditioner wouldn't run when the computer was talking. I pulled over, got out of the car and kicked the tires, because you know that would help...

John woke up now, which was a bonus since he had been sleeping since the moment we got on the road. I had no choice but to just get back in the car and start driving. I didn't need the plastic piece to keep the window up since I needed the desert air to keep myself from suffocating in the car. Even in the madness of the air and sand blowing in the car, the computer incessantly yelling what was wrong with the car, and my anger, John fell back asleep. I started having another one of my stern talks with God. I stopped for gas a while later, in the middle of nowhere, and as I was pulling back onto the road, I found myself in the back seat and the car out of control. Thank goodness no one else was driving on that road! My foot was not on the gas so it eventually came to a stop. The bolt underneath my seat had broken, because you know, enough hadn't happened already. John offered to drive, but I figured if we were going to die in my car, at least it should be me driving because, again, God was apparently really angry with me.

So, the good news is the computer shut up. Even the car knew I had reached my limit. So, we got back on the road, but I knew I couldn't let go of the steering wheel. And yes, I drove the rest of the way home like that. We made it from Sacramento, California to Lebanon, Tennessee in 54 hours. I had blisters on my hands from holding the steering wheel too tight, but we made it. I didn't go to my house—I went straight to Alecia. After I sat and cried in her arms for several hours, I fell asleep and slept for almost two days.

Facing The Past

Every time I think I am at a point it might be easier to write, I find I am completely wrong. I sat down three weeks ago to start writing this chapter, but just couldn't make myself start typing. I have contemplated, fretted, cried, and finally made myself face the fact that as much as I love my father, and as much as I want to believe that I have no anger or bitterness toward him, I do. I had a very close friend read this not long ago and I asked her for honest feedback. She came back with a list of questions, most of which centered around my dad. There are some holes up to this point about him finding his faith, how he found out about the abuse, and how he reacted. I am sitting here typing this, and honestly, I feel like I am mourning all over again. I feel like I am mourning the one relationship that I tried to keep untouched by the anger and resentment that was always nipping at my heels. I have to face the fact that there isn't a single relationship in my life that can remain untouched by the sexual abuse.

When I woke up in the safety of my sister's house, I felt like someone had dragged my dead carcass over a bed of hot coals and then let someone beat me with a two-by-four. However, I had never been happier to see her in my life! A huge part of me thought she would change her mind when I got home, but she had not. She was determined to tell Daddy, and she was convinced that she would be able to move on with her life when she did. We spent hours debating how to maneuver through the fallout afterward. We just knew Daddy would never be able to forgive Mom and we were scared what that would mean for our fragile family. I was especially worried about John. John was so private about what happened, and he had moved away so that he could move on with his life. He didn't want people to know what had happened to him, and he certainly didn't feel strong enough to look Daddy in the face. He wanted no part of the conversation but understood our need to tell him.

Alecia called Daddy and we met him at Cedar Hill Park together. I can remember sitting in her car at the park and seeing Daddy sitting at a picnic table. I sat and watched him for a few minutes before I got out of the car. Alecia kept asking me if I needed to stay in the car, but I just remember wanting to remember that moment, how he looked, before he knew. Daddy always looked so serious, and a tad bit angry. It was a protective mechanism that he had perfected to keep people from looking at him too closely. I apparently got that skill, honestly. If you didn't take the time to see the crow's feet and smile lines, or the way his beautiful green eyes danced when he smiled, you missed the beautiful softness of his face. What I saw in his face that day, all the way from the car, was worry.

I was so unsure if he would look at me differently. I had never truly seen my dad angry before. We always had such an easy relationship, and I had only been in trouble enough for a spanking one time in my whole life. He cried just as hard as I did when he spanked me. I remember him tucking me in that night as sweetly as every other night and reminding me to never let the sun set on my anger. If a heart can really break in pieces, mine was shattered by this point.

When I got out of the car and my dad saw me, he ran. He ran to me and picked me up and kissed me on the forehead so sweetly and began to cry with me. It had taken everything in him to wait those two days and let me rest. I had wondered all the way there if he knew what was going on, or why we wanted to talk to him alone. I thought that day that he had no idea, that we had blindsided him. But writing this book, I just don't know anymore. For the very first time in my life, I was quiet and I let Alecia take the lead.

I watched my dad, the strongest person I've ever known, begin to weep. He wept so openly, so hard, and for so long that we both were at a loss what to say. I had always expected some sort of righteous anger, but what I saw was heartbreak. My father had spent the last 25 years believing that he had escaped the bonds of abuse from his father and had broken the cycle and started a new family legacy of his own. What he found out instead was that his oldest son had taken the innocence of his daughters and son and that his wife had kept it from him. My dad got up from the table, he told us both that he loved us more than we could ever understand or know, and that he was sorry he didn't protect us. He told me that I was even braver than he knew, and he whispered something into Alecia's ear and walked slowly, with shaking shoulders, to his truck.

    I couldn't tell you how long Alecia and I sat in silence before we began to cry. I don't think the word cry could cover the raw outpouring of emotion that we were feeling. I was sitting there with the only person in my life who never left my side. That didn't leave me to cry alone. She held me while dealing with her own pain. We sat there for a very long time and felt utterly lost and unable to talk about what had happened. We drove in silence the hour back to her house and I got in my car (yes, the scary one that was falling apart) and I drove until I couldn't drive anymore. I pulled into a hotel a few hours away and I had what I know now was clearly a breakdown. I spent an entire week there. I didn't have anything with me, but I didn't need anything. I sat in the bed, begging for mercy, begging for anything that could take me out of the pain I was in and it was the first time I remember truly believing that killing myself was the only answer. I didn't feel like a fighter anymore, I wanted to be done and I wanted to get back in my car and drive back to Sean and beg him to take me back, but I couldn't.

I don't think when you are in that much pain, you can separate it. I couldn't tell you if I was more crushed because I had left my husband or because telling my father the truth had crushed me. The pain was so raw from both of them that I didn't know how to keep going. I had always had this inner survival instinct that kicked in for me, but it was completely MIA. I wanted to give up, I didn't want to keep running anymore, and I couldn't see that I had anything to run to. With two decades lived, I was exhausted. I was tired of fighting, tired of feeling lost and broken, and wanted out. I wrote a letter to my sister on hotel letterhead. Actually, I wrote until I ran out of paper. In my mind on that day, she was the only one who could have possibly cared that I wasn't here. I knew it would shatter her, I knew she would blame herself, but that wasn't enough for me anymore. I remember the letter almost verbatim—those words will be burned into my brain for the rest of my life.

Who Did You See?

Alecia,

No matter what I say in this letter, I can't keep this from crushing you. I can't keep you from blaming yourself, but most importantly I know I can't do this anymore. I'm tired. I'm tired of knowing that tomorrow will hurt just as much. I'm tired of knowing that no matter what I do, tomorrow is going to be just like today, and I need to be done. Always know I love you. Always know that there isn't anything you could have done. Always know that you are enough.

I drank a bottle of whiskey and I ran a tub full of water. I wish I could say that there was some sweet story of intervention or feeling covered with God's love and light, but no. I don't remember any of it. I remember waking up on the cold tile floor next to the tub with the worst hangover in the history of mankind. I apparently never made it into the tub to drown myself. Luckily, I had failed at that, too.

This was another true turning point for me. I was so furious with myself for writing that note. I was so furious with myself for being so utterly selfish and I was so furious that I was willing to let him win. I promised myself that day that I would never EVER allow myself to even consider suicide as an option. I grabbed my keys, I took a shower and washed off the whole week of wallowing in self-pity and left knowing that I had to figure out how to strengthen my own wings. There were no more secrets to hide behind and I know my mom and Damien were going to be accountable for what they had done to me. I drove home to find life just like I had left it. My dad had gone home and fallen right back in step with life. We never spoke about it for years until his final days and we never spoke about my mother's role. I don't know if he confronted her or not. I was shocked that we were back to pretending to be the perfect family.

Just like I said before when I typed about being angry, all this time I felt like if I didn't acknowledge it, that it wasn't there. It was always there lurking. I have been angry with my father since that day in the park. I wanted him to acknowledge what happened to me, for him to hold Damien and Mom accountable for how they hurt me. I wanted all the whispered promises to protect me from being hurt to boil into righteous anger at what had been taken from me. He didn't do those things. I think I excused it more than I was willing to with my mother, but it didn't mean it wasn't there. I was deeply hurt and disappointed that my father never acknowledged what I had been through.

He never confronted Damien or Mom. There was no healing from his knowledge, just more pain and disappointment. It was one more person who I loved and trusted who made the choice to not acknowledge what happened. It was swept under the rug again, and I have refused to hold him accountable until now. I wanted him to be free of any guilt in this whole mess, but unluckily he isn't. I have learned an important lesson with him. I can be angry, hold him accountable, and still love him. Being able to do that is now helping with the relationship with my mother. The silver lining here is that it did give me the insight and ability to learn to love Mom and yet keep the boundaries in place that keep me feeling safe. Learning to give them grace is giving me the space and ability to give it to myself.

Two Decades in Prison

When I was deciding how to start this chapter, I decided that Two Decades in Prison would probably be the best title to describe my second marriage. I am not sure that I can accurately describe the damage this marriage has done to me, and even more sadly, our children. I carry more guilt about this than I do anything else in my life. I have spent so much time trying to sort out how we got there, and more importantly why I chose him. It is bittersweet for me because had I not gone through this, I wouldn't have the three most important things in my life. As I was typing this, I was struck by the story about my mother telling the nurse in the hospital that she was thankful I was here. So, after I cried for a little while about how I might be turning into my mother, I smacked myself across the face and took a reality pill. I would absolutely go back and go through every painful experience to have these three children of mine. I wish that things were different for them and I wish that he would choose to be a better dad, but free will sucks.

I digress and should start back where I left off. Once upon a time there was a sad, very wounded, emotionally abused little girl who so desperately wanted something to fix. She couldn't fix any of the relationships in her own life and was on the verge of crumbling into a million broken pieces and fate brought someone into her life. Was it my ex-husband? Nope, it was his son and here is where it began.

After I left Sean, and after I was broken by my father's reaction (and by life up to that point), I started getting calls from the company that held the note on my car that was falling apart. They were trying to repo my car, so I started working two jobs to keep the wolves at bay. One of the jobs was at a movie store and that is where I met Richard. I remember the first day I worked with Richard. He was quite the sullen, emotionally absent co-worker. In fact, he got on my nerves. The manager called that night to ask me how it had gone, and I made a joke or two at Richard's expense. However, I then found out where his bad attitude was stemming from.

Richard had gone through a very tough divorce and his son was living with his mother, his ex-wife. Apparently, the mother was not taking care of him and Richard worried deeply about his son. Once again, my own brokenness was drawn to this story. I knew all too well how he must feel because of the betrayal and abandonment I felt from my relationship with my own mother. I immediately felt horrible for judging Richard and I made a point to apologize for being so rude to him.

The next day when Richard came into the store, his young son stepped out from behind him. This little boy was quite possibly the most angelic dark-haired boy I had ever seen. He had beautiful jet-black hair and he was so pale and so incredibly shy standing there holding his father's hand. I was in love with that boy. I sat there thinking about all the stories my friend told me about this beautiful little soul. Richard and I worked together again, and I listened to his story of how he had gotten where he was, and my heart broke for both of them.

Richard and Susan, Hunter's mother, went to school together. Richard graduated the year before her. They were madly in love and Susan got pregnant with Hunter. Although they were young, he was determined to make it work and had done everything he could. He even moved into the basement of his in-laws' house, but she didn't want to stay married. Hunter was severely asthmatic and had been in and out of the hospital repeatedly during his short four years of life. I thought about his beautiful ruby red lips and shy smile the whole time Richard relayed this story to me. I certainly connected with the sadness he must have felt from having a mother who was more concerned with herself than his needs.

Richard left a sweet card in my car the following day while I worked thanking me for

Who Did You See?

listening to him. He wanted to take me on a date. I remember sitting at Baskin Robbins and listening to more and more stories and feeling so sorry for him, but more importantly, knowing that his sweet little boy deserved so much more. Things progressed very quickly with Richard, because that was apparently how I rolled. Sorry, I just couldn't resist. Looking back, I was more drawn to Hunter because there was finally something I could fix. I could help Richard get custody of him. I could help this boy whose mother wasn't putting him first.

From the beginning our relationship was very tumultuous. We both were suffering from our past failed relationships and you certainly have heard my story, so you know I had some deep demons. Richard had a whole set of demons of his own, and I had no idea what I was dealing with. I disregarded his manipulation and jealousy, as I thought I had found someone who just loved me so much he couldn't help himself. We would break up and then end up making up again. It was a vicious cycle. Although he knew there were issues at home with my mom, he didn't know for a while how deep and terrible those things were.

Richard was so jealous that once when we broke up, I went out on a date with someone else, only to find him sitting outside on the front of his car waiting for us to leave the movie and he caused a scene. I should have taken cues from the "I may not want you, but no one else can have you" attitude, but I did not. It got to the point that we needed to make a choice to figure out how to make it work or just break it off completely. We sat by the lake in Hendersonville talking about why it wasn't working for us, and I burst into tears. I bared my soul to him about everything that had happened to me as a child, about my mom knowing, but not the whole story about Sean. I just couldn't share that pain with anyone else. He was stunned. I could see him almost recoil from how ugly the story was to him. You see, his family were good people—at least, if you didn't look too closely.

He has a huge, close-knit family. Richard is the oldest of four children. They lived in a big, beautiful house in the suburbs and he had lived a much more charmed life than I had lived. His father had always done well financially, and his mother stayed home doting on her four children. When we first met, his father was running for office and we were attending fundraisers and exciting events. It was all so foreign to me, and I loved that his family was so "normal." They represented everything that my family wasn't, and I had this idea that they would accept me and love me like their own. That, however, was a wish that didn't come true. What I seemed to miss is that no matter what, blood is always thicker than water, and much thicker than right or wrong.

Richard and I wed in February 1994 in Gatlinburg. All of our family drove to the mountains and I had hoped that I would live happily ever after. I went back and looked at all of our pictures before I started writing this chapter. There is one photograph I haven't been able to get out of my mind. Someone captured Alecia and me in a sisterly conversation. I am brushing her hair away from her face and one would assume from the look on our faces that we are having a sweet conversation. What that frame really caught was her telling me that it wasn't too late to run. You see, Alecia was feeling a deep hole of regret because she felt like she had pushed me into marrying him. Richard and I had set the wedding date because of a blow-up that Alecia and I had about the two of us living together and not being married. To understand that fight you have to understand Alecia a little better. She managed to maneuver the abuse with much more finesse than I did. She still seemed to hold onto her innocence in a way that I not only respected, but very much envied.

She still "saved herself" for her future husband. She still managed to love and respect Mom. She kept working on forgiving Damien, and most of all, she still respected herself. She never understood my self-destructive behavior, and although she loved me more than anyone else in my life, she was always furious with my behavior and confused by my lack of respect for myself. I never felt judged by her, although in retrospect, I know it was impossible for her not to. Even without the blinders of true love for this woman, you need to know she was stunningly beautiful. She was as opposite of me in every way she could be, both on the inside and out.

I was always tall, lanky, and fair as a baby's butt; she was shorter, curvaceous, and soaked up all the Native American genes. She had smoldering dark eyes and a beautiful complexion and had people not heard us laugh, they would never have believed we were sisters. She never excused my behavior, but she loved me so much that once she said her peace, she moved on. She knew me well enough to know that when I made a decision, it was made. That was so evident and represented in the picture someone snapped at dinner after the wedding ceremony. She was there supporting and loving me as always, but looked me square in the face and said, "You know, beautiful, it isn't too late to get out of here." I brushed the hair away from her face and she said, "You know he doesn't love you like you deserve; he loves the idea of you." As always, my sister was right.

Who Did You See?

Richard and I were never meant to withstand the difficulties of being together forever. I think a lot about how my life would have been different if I had listened to my sister or if I had a mother who cared more about my decisions in my life. Regardless, as things solidified in our roles together, Hunter's home life continued to fall apart. In looking back now, I honestly don't know how to separate what Richard and his family told me from what is the truth. I believe Richard married me for this exact situation and we never paused before filing for emergency custody of his son. We were awarded custody, and the boy I fell in love with at the movie store was now my responsibility.

There are probably more books about me trying to parent him with no idea what the hell I was doing, all while trying to learn how to be a wife to the most textbook narcissist I have ever met. Everyone knows that hindsight is so much clearer, but I wish I had paid attention to how he took such pleasure in watching Hunter's mother suffer.

It wasn't that this marriage was not what I expected. It wasn't that I was now parenting a child who wasn't mine or that I had no idea what I was doing, and it wasn't that I was still putting band-aids on all the emotional wounds that needed greater attention. It certainly wasn't that Richard only loved me on his own terms. It was all of these things and so much more. I was only valued in this marriage by Richard's terms.

    I think it is important for all of you to know what those 20 years took from me, but I am not sure that it is the time to document the whole story. Having young children, the specifics are probably for another time. I can sum up the entire two decades with a few insights. By Richard's own words, he explained why he should have been allowed to abuse me. Do you remember the story a few paragraphs back about me bearing my soul in the car to him about the abuse I had endured? Well, every time we fought or he was trying to get me to forgive him this was his rationale, "Pam, I have been patient with you. Most men would have walked away from you when they found out you were damaged goods. I could have driven off at the lake, but I didn't. I stayed and so you know I love you."

    So that is my life with Richard, in summary. I stayed, dying a little more every single day. For Richard, I was nothing more than visible representation of his ability to love something that was damaged. I was there for Richard's benefit, whatever that looked like to him, so I convinced myself to stay over and over and over and over until I couldn't stay anymore. I endured all the emotional abuse, his cheating, and his tearful apologies. I had chosen someone exactly like my mother. Someone who only found value in how I fulfilled what he needed, and what he wanted. I chose someone who I knew would let me down because it couldn't hurt if I didn't expect anything else. I was wrong again—it did hurt.

I had children with a man who couldn't love me or my children the way that we needed because he was too selfish to see past his own wants and needs. Yes, I chose a spouse just like my mother, the one person who I always felt betrayed me the most.

Hunter

Oddly enough, I found a very comfortable rhythm to parenting. I had no idea what a good mother looked like; I never intended on being a parent. However, I loved that I had a chance to play a new role. I saw this like every other role I decided to play. In my mind, I wasn't deep or whole enough to actually be someone who could do this for real, I just had to play the part the best I could, and no one would care or see the difference. I wanted to be Hunter's whole life because his situation with a selfish mother felt familiar to me. I thought that this was the opportunity to heal my own wounds by being what I really needed and never had. Looking back now, I think in some ways I failed miserably.

My good intentions didn't always translate into my actions—not in the way you would think. I am not the one who has great ideas but doesn't have the fortitude to follow through with them. It is the exact opposite. I follow through; I follow through like gangbusters. I follow through to the point that people beg me to stop. The bigger problem with that is that I don't accept or understand why others aren't doing the same thing. I hold everyone to such a standard that no one could ever live up to it. I wanted to be the parent that Hunter would grow up and say, "Oh my

Lord, what would I have done if Pam hadn't come along to save me?" The problem with that is that it doesn't leave a lot of room for him to openly love his mother or share his feelings of where he is or what he needs. It was about me and not about him, and my heart aches for all that lost time and for hurting him. My intentions were good, my delivery not so much. The bull in a china shop has nothing on me.

Between my need to parent him to death and his father's need to punish his mother, we weren't the parents we wanted to be or that he needed us to be. Neither of us were emotionally healthy enough to see past what we were doing, and now I can see what our actions cost that sweet, beautiful boy. I wanted him to not need his mother, to know what we were sacrificing and be thankful. Instead he was hurt, he was angry, and he was wounded. I should have recognized that, but I didn't at the time. In spite of that, he was an amazing son. He was a great student, he was a good child and beyond the normal teenage and rebellious antics, he made our life easier than he should have. Although we seemed to be in constant battle with his mother, he was not the source of our anguish or fighting. I wish I had stopped to enjoy what a blessing he was to me then and I will always be incredibly sorry for that.

Hunter always had such a servant's heart. He was a good friend and was the first to come to the defense of someone he loved. That will always be one of the things that I love most about him. He wanted approval from his father so badly that he would do whatever we wanted him to do, with all his heart. He struggled with asthma, but out on the football field every coach would talk about his heart to play. Hunter surrounded himself with good friends, and I was always proud that he seemed to have such a strong sense of who he was, whether we understood it or not. He was very close to his mother and her family. Much closer than he was to us or Richards's family. He loved us and he loved them, but there was a connection there that was always pulling him, and we felt betrayed rather than understanding or being proud of his desire to protect them from our attacks.

Hunter is a happily married man, he is a good husband and a good father. He doesn't choose to be part of my life and I will always feel a huge void in my life. I hope that he learns to forgive me, and I hope that someday things will be different. Until that time, I will continue to pray for him and continue to hope for more. This is a repeating pattern of my life that I give much more grace to people than I ever get back.

FREEDOM

When I tell people the story of coming out of that marriage, it surprises them that I compare it to Mel Gibson in Braveheart yelling FREEDOM! It defies logic that a 38-year-old woman with three children, a stressful career, and taking in her mother would describe it in such terms. Most people describe the ending of a marriage that long as a death. They need time to mourn the loss of what could have been. I never saw it in those terms. I had been so incredibly unhappy for so long. I had been finding myself feeling smaller and more invisible every day. I didn't feel valued for who I was, and I felt like I had no voice in my marriage. I had tried to leave so many times that the idea of breaking away and raising my children on my own felt like my only alternative.

I am going to leave most of the story of Richard and me for a time when it will have less impact on the kids, but I do think hearing the story of him and his children is appropriate. It was a very rough road for the children, and no matter how I tried to make it easier, the fact that I didn't want to take their father back is something that I have already had to answer for. He is remarried, but routinely sits Krista down and says to her that he still loves me, will always love me, and didn't want this divorce. This is very confusing for the kids, to sit and endure that conversation with his new wife. Richard's concept of love is different from that of any person I have ever known. He seems to believe that his actions are always justified if he "does it in love." He doesn't seem to care much if his actions are in the best interest of the receiver. Again, I picked my mother in a man's body.

When we first separated, he moved next door with his parents. Although he was a few acres away, he had no interest in spending any time with the kids. He didn't take any visitation with them until he was ordered to by our parenting plan. He was living next door for several months and then a few miles away for a year and a half. Although he "stopped by," he didn't take them overnight or for any visitation outings until we finalized an agreement. I never understood completely why, but there always seemed to be a need for me to beg him to spend time with the kids. He wanted to hurt me by hurting the kids. As you can imagine, the visits were very tumultuous because they had never really spent any time away with him by themselves and he has never been known to be patient with them.

I can remember one weekend not long after he started visitation that still brings me to tears. Krista called me and was almost inconsolable. She was whispering and crying and was begging me to come get her. She was scared because it was storming. She kept telling me she couldn't go to Richard's room because he would yell at her. I kept encouraging her to go to him and tell him that she was scared, but she wouldn't do it. She wouldn't make herself vulnerable because she said that the last time she went into his room at night, he yelled at her. I sat on the floor, wiping away my own tears while I talked to her about the beach until she drifted off to sleep. I sat with the phone in my hand listening to her steady breathing for about an hour before I hung up. I felt helpless and sad, and absolutely riddled with guilt. I knew what it felt like to be held captive, fearing Richard's reaction and the inevitable wrath that would follow.

The kids would alternate between being excited to see him, worried what would happen, and upset that they couldn't have the same relationship they have with me. It is and always has been a very difficult situation for them. No matter how badly I wanted to move on, he wanted difficulty to engulf me. There would be no peace. If his parents were at the kids' games, they would insult me loudly enough for everyone in the stands to hear. He would barrage me with emails that were completely insulting and fight me on every single thing that he could.

On one particular weekend, I was across town with someone I had just started seeing. I got a call from Richard and he was yelling at the kids as I answered the phone. He was taking them to the house and leaving them. When I told him I was not home, he said he didn't care. He was "leaving YOUR kids there"—he couldn't deal with them anymore. I sped across town as fast as humanly possible to find him standing in the driveway. As I jumped out of the car, he opened his truck door, grabbed Jack from the seat, and literally threw him into my arms. He was yelling and screaming, all the kids were crying, and he sped off, leaving tracks on the road and saying he had no intention of taking the kids for visitation anymore. The fight had started over something about me. Richard was fighting with Alec, and of course, it turned into a fight about me. Alec, taking up for me, ended up bringing the problems with his dad to a head. From that point on, there was a distinct change in their relationship from which they never fully recovered. Richard found how to rile Alec up, and sadly, I feel like that was the pattern that he put on repeat where Alec is concerned.

To understand why, you need to understand that Richard had been telling me since Alec was a toddler that I was "ruining Alec." Since Alec was such a mommy's boy, and he was attached to me like glue, that, in his words, I was "making him gay like my brother." He called him names, he tormented him when he could and encouraged his family to do the same. His parents took every opportunity to compare him to their other grandchildren because he was going to turn out like his mother. I couldn't do anything right in their eyes and now, neither could my son. There was the constant torment that he would never amount to anything. He and Alec seemed to fall into the same abusive pattern as our marriage and it turned Alec inside out. His father and family would wind him up like a toy and seemed to take pleasure in watching him spiral out of control. Alec would end up doing something destructive and then Richard and his family would point their finger and say, "I told you so!"

Krista and Jack were so small and scared that they wouldn't dare upset their dad because they saw how he treated Alec. So, the pattern of abuse started with all of them. They all love their father, but they are so much like me that they struggle the same way I did. It is painful to watch and always makes me feel guilty for bringing them into the situation. I have certainly made plenty of mistakes, but I try very hard to encourage them to love him anyway. I want them to find something to love in their father and love it fiercely. I want them to love it unconditionally and have peace with him.

Things were in absolute turmoil living so close to Richard and his family. I was debating about our future because I knew I didn't want Alec attending the high school there. He was in a kindergarten through eighth grade school and I knew I wanted to move but had no idea where or how. I had started to date and had found my groove again, to put it lightly. I had shut myself down for 20 years to stay in that marriage and it literally felt like I was beginning to come alive again. I met one of the most amazing men that graced my life during that time. Bill and his daughter were there during a time that I am not sure I could have maneuvered alone. We fell right into step and I adored his daughter, Erin, as much as I adored him. Bill never seemed to let the drama with Richard bother him. He had his own crazy ex-wife so he just laughed about it and poured me a whiskey when I needed it, which was often.

I spent 18 months with him and have some of the fondest memories. I had felt dead for two decades and Bill was a perpetual teenager. You couldn't help but have fun with him as he finds humor in everything. He made me laugh, made me feel young again and helped me to forget that my life was in constant turmoil. His daughter brought immeasurable joy to me and was the first person brought into my life who I didn't feel like I needed to save. She, like her father, made you feel calm just to be in their presence. They insulated me from the madness that was going on in my life and I love them to this day for it.

As with every other time in my life, I couldn't seem to be alone. I fell from one bad relationship to another and if it wasn't causing me drama, it scared me, and I ran from it. Unluckily, I ran from Bill and into another EPIC mistake.

Husband Number 3

I met husband number 3 in the line of duty. Let's just call him "Gill." I met him the first time when I was working at a medical practice and we busted one of my nurses for prescription drug fraud. He was 9 years younger and I was in the middle of the separation with Richard. He was a drug task agent, and although we dated for a few months, he was bothered that the divorce wasn't final and that I had no intentions at the time of moving closer. We broke things off and I met Bill and all was right with the world. I moved medical practices and one day out of the blue in walked Gill. He texted me that he was in the lobby and when I brought him back to introduce him to the physicians that I worked for, he announced that he was there because he was going to marry me. I remember laughing and thinking maybe he had started taking drugs himself.

For a week, every day, he gave me a new reason as to why we were getting married. He knew I didn't want Alec to attend the high school where we were, and he knew the chaos that Richard created for the kids and for me. I remember sitting there with him at a restaurant after work at the end of the week and thinking I must have lost my mind. Here is this intelligent, handsome, Christian man who wants to be a father to my kids. He wants to give us a chance to start over and he is trying to sweep me off my feet. I felt like Julia Roberts in Pretty Woman (although I wasn't a hooker). All I had to do was say yes, break things off with Bill, and I could finally have someone to take some of the burden off my shoulders. He was convinced he could handle Richard and that when Richard saw that the kids were happy and settled, he wouldn't mess with him. Just typing that makes me laugh.

I so badly wanted to start over. I wanted someone to be there for me. I felt alone in the world with no family (other than my mom) and I was becoming more and more exhausted fighting with Richard all the time. Between working full-time and having no help with the kids, I felt like I was being offered a lifeline. So, you guessed it. We got married in May 2012, and I moved in with Gill and started a new life. I fell for it, hook, line, and sinker. Gill took Alec on a long walk after I accepted his proposal to ask for my hand, since he was the "man" of the house. He promised my son to always treat me with respect and promised to be the role model that Alec was lacking. Alec had already begun to give me a difficult time before Gill walked into our life. His eighth-grade year had been hard on both of us because he was finding his rebellious side. When Gill showed Alec respect, a light went off in him and he wanted to prove to him that he was worthy of his respect. Things were changing for us! We all said goodbye to what had been our life and moved an hour away to start over with someone who we believed loved us like no one ever had.

Gill painted such a perfect picture to the outside world. He had such an important job, he was a strong Christian man, he loved his daughter and stepdaughter, and took care of his ex-wife. He didn't fight with her; he seemed to treasure the role she filled for his daughter. He didn't torment her like Richard did me and he was so involved in her life because he understood how important it was to be there for her. We were all so excited to have some stability and security in our life that the kids were openly making changes and accepting new rules without much struggle at all. I woke up every morning thanking God that he had sent such an answer to us.

While moving in, I noticed his daughter and ex-wife (who lived two doors down) didn't seem very excited about us being there. I rationalized how difficult it must be for his ex-wife to see a new woman and her children taking her place and my heart truly broke for her. I reached out to her, sat down and poured out my heart about all we had been through, hoping she would see that I was not a threat to her and her daughter. His daughter didn't want to spend time with us or stay at our house. She was always pleasant when her dad was there, but the minute he was not, she was a totally different person. She was very passive-aggressive, and things were certainly not going like I had hoped. Compared to our old life, this was nothing, so I laughed about how stressful my friends would talk about living two doors down from his ex-wife might be.

Then the real fun began. Richard had been eerily quiet, lurking, waiting for the right moment to attack. Alec was settling in to his new school, he was playing football, and flourishing in our new community and home. Krista had found a new best friend next door, and Jack had made his very first best friend at daycare. Their dad would call, the kids wouldn't answer, and it was simply because they were having so much fun. Gill was a stickler for the rules, to say the least. He had a very strict "policy" about everything. He expected the house to be kept in complete order -- all the time. With a house full of kids that wasn't easy, so I found myself scrubbing baseboards, making homemade laundry soap (at his insistence), vacuuming, and polishing the floors constantly. He created a checklist for the kids to complete daily, which I agreed with completely. The problem was that if they checked something and it wasn't done to his standards there was hell to pay. He began to insist they were all liars because if they didn't do it 150%

that they had lied to him about doing it. The less time his daughter spent there, the more he seemed to find reasons to punish them and be unhappy with whatever they, or I, was doing. Then since his daughter didn't feel comfortable staying there, he had to spend the night at his ex-wife's house.

Things went from bad to worse on both fronts. His family didn't want us there, and Richard began to attack in every way he could. He was picking fights with Gill at Alec's football games, accusing Gill of being around while Krista was changing, sending me crazy emails, and calling and picking fights constantly. Then he began calling Gill's boss and accused him of having an affair with me while we were still married, and alleged he threatened him with his gun at a football game. As if blending families wasn't hard enough, he gave us NO peace. Then, he called the Department of Human Services, because he was concerned about his children. That was the final straw—Gill snapped. He began to pick on all of us in return, relentlessly. Although I had warned him tirelessly before we started this about Richard and how I knew he would torment us, he believed he could handle him. After all, he dealt with criminals every day!

Well, he couldn't deal with Richard. He couldn't take the embarrassment at work. He couldn't handle that his daughter wasn't accepting us. He didn't like that the kids wouldn't completely shut out their own father. He was angry that he was sacrificing for them and they were still choosing their father over him.

All of a sudden, I had become his enemy. I had brought all this into his life, and worse, into his daughter's life. I somehow became untrustworthy. I became someone who he couldn't even look at, much less love or adore. In an instant, my whole life fell apart. I had given up everything to move there. I had no furniture of my own, I was in his house, I had taken a job with less stress and hence much less money to be more available at home, I had nothing but Gill. Guess what? He didn't want me anymore, unless I was willing to send Alec to his father's house. You see, he began to attack Alec because Alec was the only person in the house he could. Alec was a teenager, doing teenage things and Gill wouldn't have any of that.

Alec could do nothing right. If Alec didn't have straight A's, he was grounded. If he didn't make his bed or do the list like Gill wanted, he was grounded. If he cursed or didn't live up to being the man of the house when Gill was at work, he was grounded. When he was changing after taking a shower in his own room and didn't close the blinds, the crazy bus driver called the police and accused him of flashing her. Gill lost his mind and Alec was going to be the end of his entire life. We began to constantly fight about Alec. He wanted me to send him to his father's house, and he was going to stop at nothing until it happened. He tried to get Alec to hit him. He would get in Alec's face and taunt him, and then tell me that I wasn't worthy of him and his daughter because I had created this.

I had lost everything in a blink of an eye. I had gone against everyone in my life who kept telling me to wait, not to rush into this. He had absolutely strategically cut everyone off in my life because I needed to focus on establishing the family that I had been unable to do before on my own. He made me believe in all of his promises, and even worse, I had let him take advantage of my mom. When we moved to Spring Hill, we moved her there too. We found her an apartment close enough to us so we could watch over her. She felt the warmth of the love he so freely gave in the beginning and was just as thankful to have some security, the first feeling of security since my father had died. She still owned the house I grew up in, but it was literally falling apart. The renters were a nightmare; it was in an area of town where property values were rapidly decreasing, the maintenance issues were eating up all the rent, and none of us could deal with it anymore.

Who Did You See?

Gill had made room in his little house for us but had run out of money to finish the upstairs. Mom had noticed the strain that was happening between us, and Alec had confided in her about what was happening between Richard and Gill. She knew better than most the havoc that their father could cause in our life, and she had seen the evil person he became with me, more than once. She was worried for us, and so when Gill sat down with her and asked her to sell her house, she listened to him and trusted him because I did.

He had it all worked out, he knew her health would be declining, and she would need assistance, and so if he invested the money into finishing the house it would "fix all the problems" for all of us. He could create a space for Alec and his daughter upstairs. He was going to teach Alec responsibility by having him help work on it, try to get things on track with him. It would give his daughter a place to help her bond with us, and in return, he promised to always take care of Mom. He held her hand and looked into her eyes and said that all of us would always be able to lean on him and we would never have to worry about feeling safe again. She agreed to give him the money to finish the house and for the very first time in my life, I saw my mom be completely selfless. It affected me in a way I don't know how to explain—

most of all because I felt like it wasn't because of me, it was because of him.

If there was a way I could hit reverse and go back to this moment in time, I would give just about anything I own to do so. If I had known what he was going to do, if I had known how dishonest and manipulative he was, I would beg Mom not to do it. I understand now, what he had been doing all along. We were just pawns for him. He had moved to that house, two doors down, to establish a new life with his daughter. He wanted to prove to them, and to his ex-wife, that he could make up for all that he done to them. You see, he cheated on her. He had abandoned his family years before, and everything about his life now was about proving that he was worthy of a new start. It was so important that everyone know that he was "taking in this broken family and in doing so redeeming himself." He had a perfect out, because he could blame it all on Richard and Alec. I had a crazy ex-husband and troubled teenage son, so it wouldn't be his fault at all.

So, yes, you guessed it. He threw himself into finishing his home. He attended every single event with the children, pasted on a smile, and layered on promises and a show of faith. As he finished the house, his trips away to see his daughter and ex-wife increased and so did his hours at work. He didn't want to be at home with us. As he spent more time away, he became more and more vocal about how Alec and I were not trustworthy. We couldn't do anything right. In Gill's words, "neither of us were worthy of the time and energy he had invested in us." Mom was never welcome anymore, because Gill said she undermined him with the children. Our lives had completely and utterly unraveled.

As Alec started to overhear our arguments, the tension grew much, much worse. Gill would profess me as Queen, and above reproach. He would profess that women were to be revered and honored, but behind closed doors he would do the opposite. Alec began to see that he didn't practice what he preached. Alec began to stick up for me and in doing so he put a final nail in his own coffin. When Richard saw a crack, he began to pour as much water down it as possible. His attacks on Gill and me got more frequent. Eventually, Gill could take no more. Gill wanted a divorce, he wanted us out of his house, and I had nowhere to go and no one to turn to, so I tried everything I could to convince him to make it work.

Then the attacks got much more volatile. Alec borrowed Gill's favorite pen out of our desk. Alec had used it, and Gill completely tore Alec's room apart looking for it. When I got home from the grocery store, he and Alec were yelling at each other on the front porch. He was swinging at Alec and I thought he was going to kill him. I got out of the car and tried to break them apart, but Gill began swinging at both of us and had completely snapped. I pulled Alec away and Gill went into the house and started throwing all of Alec's things in the front yard. We got in the car and I was trying to calm him down, but all I could think about was running away; but to where? We had nowhere to go.

    Gill texted me and said "that animal was not welcome in HIS home." He said I could return without him and pack his things to take him to his father permanently. Our marriage was over that day. There was no coming back from that. He began to change the door lock to a new code every day. The kids couldn't get in "his house" unless I was home. When he was home, we were all scared of him. The kids were afraid of him, and he was absolutely taunting Alec. Then, the following day Krista got off the bus, and he had changed the code again. She was on the porch, I was stuck in traffic, and she began to have an asthma attack on the front porch. When I called him and was explaining what was happening, he laughed. He had won. He was going to get us out of his house. Between his maniacal laugh and his absolute disregard for her health, I knew I had to protect us from him. I went to my attorney and got a restraining order.

Pamela Chastain

Starting Over – Again

There are not words that I can put on this paper to explain what this did to me. I cannot fully explain how utterly lost, devastated, and broken I was. We were all devastated, and I had no idea what I was going to do. I didn't know this man, I was scared to death of him and I was even more scared of what this was doing to my children. Richard had won, my chance of a happy marriage was over and done. Would Gill have snapped if Richard had left us alone? Was this who he really was? Why did he do this? Where would we go?

I was actually scared for myself. I began to get sick, very sick. I couldn't eat. I couldn't sleep. I was afraid Richard would come after the kids. I was scared that Gill would come after me for ruining his career. I didn't know what I had done to him to make him hate me this much. We had been talking to our pastor about helping us with our marriage, and so I reached out to him to tell him what had happened. He suggested that I join his wife's bible study group. They were an amazing group of women, and it might help to surround myself with people who could love and support me. I went that week, and what a gift they were. They were the most diverse group of women you could imagine and they took me in. They not only let me join their group, but they prayed with and for me. They

Who Did You See?

listened while I cried, I worried, I prayed that God would soften Gill's heart toward us. I just couldn't face another divorce, another failure. I couldn't face the idea that I had been so wrong about him, and what he felt for me and my kids. There must be something I didn't know. I must be due a miracle, right?

I was praying for a way to fix something that was never meant to be. I was praying for God to soften someone's heart who I believe never had good intentions toward me or my kids. I wavered constantly between being incredibly angry and utterly broken. I tried my best to put on a brave face for my children, but absolutely wanted to give up. The worst part was Richard's cocky smile when I encountered him for the first time after he found out Gill wanted a divorce. When the kids are older, and I can write more about what that man put me through, you'll understand what that unleashed in me. A friend always says there is a special place in hell for him. That nagging feeling of hopelessness would have certainly found a welcome home in my heart had those women not surrounded me with God's love. They prayed with me, for me, and loved on me and, once again, saved my life.

Gill wanted his badge and gun back and the only way to get it was to get me to drop the restraining order. I spent a lot of time praying to forgive him for what he put us through, and I spent a lot of time praying about what to do. One day he would be trying to get me to talk to him and the next he wanted to move the divorce forward. Ironically, when we finally sat down to talk it was on the porch of his mother's condominium looking out on the pond where we were married. I was so incredibly hopeful and in love that day two short years before. I wasn't scared at all. I felt like God had finally taken mercy on me. I was smiling so hard all day that my face was sore for days. I sat there while we both cried and talked about a way to find our way back and I knew sitting there that it couldn't be done. His daughter hated me, my ex-husband would never give us peace, my son knew he wasn't who he professed to be, and I knew he didn't love me. He loved the idea of what I represented for him. I really cannot profess to know his heart, but what I do know, is that he isn't who I believed him to be. He hurt me in a way I had never let anyone hurt me because I didn't make him earn my trust, it was freely given. I have seen the quote many times from Bob Marley, "the biggest coward of a man is to awaken the love of a woman without the intention of loving her" and I always feel like it was written for him.

So, we went forward with the divorce, we moved into a new home and we started a new life—again. I could see how worried the kids were for me,

Who Did You See?

and I put on the bravest face I have ever mustered. I was barely surviving paying all the bills, I had moved my mother back in with me, and I was as lost as I had ever been. I could see that Mom was drinking again, and I knew that things were spiraling out of control. I fell back into the same behavior of my youth. I didn't see any of my value, and I was lonely, so I gave myself to anyone who was interested. When the kids were with their father, I was drinking. I was drinking and dating a lot and I was not thinking about anything but what I needed to get through one day at a time. I needed to feel wanted, I needed to feel like someone found me worthy and, just like in my youth, I gave myself freely to people who recognized my brokenness.

The day of our mediation, I left and drove across town and had sex in my car with someone in a snowstorm. I have found myself trying to rationalize that statement, but there is no rationalization of my behavior for that day or the months following. I was dating so many people that I couldn't possibly have found time to have feelings for any of them. I made sure they were all men that were emotionally unavailable and if I thought they had any interest at all in me, I cut them off. I would joke about having been right about what men were good for decades before and I quit going to church and to my bible study. I didn't want to think about what God thought about me anymore. I felt betrayed by Him. I felt like every time I let Him in, He let people hurt me. I did a lot of shaking my fist at God, like always.

Then the one consistent pattern in my life fell into place again. I saw all the signs of my mother spinning out of control again. This is always the story. When someone else was hurting or needing her, she retreated into herself and into her bottle. This was always followed by some health crisis or "accident" so I had to pull myself together to prepare for what I knew was coming. I started not answering the texts and requests from the all the men I was seeing. I put down my own bottle and I pulled out my Bible. I had something happen then that I wasn't prepared for just yet. I wanted to write; I wanted to journal.

I started writing, not about any of this, but about what I was reading about in the Bible. I had always refused to write, other than in school. Writing things down made them real to me. I didn't think I had the strength to deal with anything in my life. My life was always about "pulling up my boot straps" and just dealing with the latest crisis. I wasn't ready to journal about what happened, but I was ready to just write about what those passages were saying to me. I found comfort going back to the passages that I had studied months before. I wrote in my Bible under Romans Chapter 9, "I am

Who Did You See?

not an accident, I was formed by God with His purpose". Romans speaks to me because Paul is speaking about present suffering for future glory. That spoke so deeply to where I felt like I was stuck for so many years. All the passages that I highlighted during that women's Bible study were a constant reminder to me that I was meant for greatness.

> "I consider that our present sufferings are not worth comparing with the glory that will be revealed in us." (Romans 8:28)

> "And we know that in all things God works for the good of those who love Him, who have been called according to his purpose." (Romans 8:18)

I always had a running "fight" with my dad about a few things, but one of them was about my relationship with God. I have already told you how my dad loved to pick verbal fights with me just to "prepare me" for life. He loved to pick the opposite side of fights to get me to think through my arguments. This wasn't one of those things. He truly disagreed with me on it, but always listened to me and respected that I was so passionate about it. I believe that my walk with God has to be utterly, completely, and beautifully unique. I don't think that either my relationship or my path that I walk with Him can be like anyone else's. If I believe that God made me unique and unlike anyone else, He can't expect that my relationship can be like anyone else. If I believe that to be true, than I also have to believe that how He speaks, how He responds, how He shows his love has to be unique, too.

I believe that God has a sense of humor. I believe that He knows that is how I need Him to speak to me and He loves me enough to love me where I am, even if it doesn't "please Him." I believe my relationship with God has been the one consistent, but always changing, thing in my life. I believed growing up that God expected me to be as perfect as a human could be. I believed that He was only hearing me when I was where He wanted me to be. I don't believe that was taught to me in Sunday school or church; but I think we hear more from where we are in our life than what we are actually being told. I wanted to hide from Him the places that hurt the most, but what He wanted was to love me there. Love me enough to heal it, but I just wasn't ready to let Him. It is so strange for me to type this now because I have spent my whole adult life telling people that I want to love people where they are, not where I want them to be. When people called me for advice, I said those words over and over and over. I believe with my whole heart that is how God loves me. That realization changed me. It changed my expectation of what that relationship looked like and in turn began to change how every single relationship in my life looked to me. First and foremost, the one that brought me the most pain, the one with my mom.

Pamela Chastain

Are We Different?

As I started to watch my mother's pattern of destruction, I compared it to my own. I tried to talk to her; I reached out for the first time to try to tell her that this didn't make any sense. She had thrown away all the time we had together. She had wasted the time with her grandkids, now choosing to love herself and her vodka more than looking for a way to deal with all the pain. She was living with us, but never left her room or wanted anything to do with any of us. When the kids were gone for the weekend, she was so drunk she could barely walk. I reached out, but she denied that she was even drinking. She looked at me with such anger and disgust when she was drinking. It felt like I was the reason for all her pain in her own mind. She had blamed me for years for being the one who challenged her and wanted people to know what happened to us. I took up time with Daddy, whom she wanted for herself. I never loved her the way she thought I should. I was never grateful for what she thought were sacrifices. I didn't make any attempt to understand all her pain and the destruction she came from. Most of all, I let Gill take advantage of her. There was no reaching her—all I could do was watch it play out.

The more she spiraled out of control, I fell into the pattern of putting myself back together. I

Who Did You See?

knew this time had to be different, so I didn't pretend. I didn't throw on my mask and put on my Wonder Woman costume. I didn't want it to be just another time that I was grabbing for my boot straps. I didn't want to end up like my mother. But, was I any different? I was just as destructive to myself; it just wasn't as messy. I needed to be different for myself as well as my kids. I needed to mirror a different woman for my daughter and be a better example of what my sons would look for in a partner. Outwardly I did a great job of putting that mask on, but I took it off in private. I was self-destructive. I was broken. I was scared. I was alone. I was hurting so deeply that my chest hurt to take a deep breath. I had a decision to make now that I was peeling back the layers. Do I stop, call my therapist, and go do what I had always done and put a band-aid on it? Or, do I chance peeling a few layers back and chance being right about not being able to face it?

    I literally got on my knees. I prayed harder than I had ever prayed in my life. I prayed on and off for an entire weekend while the kids were gone. Maybe I should be honest; they weren't like any prayers that I was taught. They wouldn't have looked like prayers to anyone who saw me. I talked to God for the very first time in my life. Once I let that floodgate open, I couldn't stop it. I let Him have it at first. Not like all the fist-shaking of the past, but I absolutely laid out my case. I shared every single memory that bubbled up.

I prayed not just for that little girl, but for whoever else was in that memory. I found myself praying for my brother who had hurt me so deeply, I prayed for my mother and how helpless she must have felt. I prayed for my dad because I knew how much he loved me and I realized how many tears he must have shed in a room like this asking God why. I prayed for the kids' father and his family. I prayed for my friends, who were more like family who had never abandoned me when they should have run from all the drama my crazy life had created. I prayed for all the people who I knew I had disappointed. I prayed for all the people who I had hurt, who my destructive behavior had led astray. I prayed for forgiveness, but, most importantly, I begged for strength not to go back to pretending. If I needed to fall apart I was willing to, just so I could really heal. I prayed and prayed and prayed to help me not put on my mask again. I wanted to be seen. No longer could I make a version of me for someone else. I wanted to peel away every single layer and show myself and everyone else in my life who I was.

I thought I had been tired at other times in my life. In fact, I felt like I had been tired my entire life. There was an exhaustion following that weekend that lasted for days. I was absolutely spent. I picked up the kids and knew that the most important battle of my life was beginning because I would have to battle myself to stay in that place. I was a worthy adversary, and this would be a constant battle for me to change. When the kids worriedly asked me if I was okay, I started with honesty with them. I didn't say, "Of course, baby, I'm great." It was as simple as saying, "I will be."

With every simple change in the beginning, I felt a little more at peace. Giving up the idea of control for me always seemed to be too overwhelming. Funny, it was the easiest thing I have ever done. It became easier every day to get up with the expectation that I only had to be where I was. No one needed me to pretend to be a warrior, and if they did we would have to change that expectation. I found that in looking at my intentions, I think I was more like my mother than I realized. I didn't want to be here any more than she did; every action and every inaction was hurting me, not only emotionally, but physically. My health had never been great but the stress of the last few years had eaten away at me and I never did anything to make it better.

I had to get my health back on track. I went to the gym, hired a personal trainer, and went for my very first complete physical ever. I went to the doctor like I went to the therapist, just when I thought I was going to die! Let me be very clear, the stress in my life didn't get any better. I was still dealing with my mother who was repeating her old patterns of bad behavior. I was still raising a teenager, who was trying his best to kill me with stress. I still couldn't cover all my bills. I was still dealing with the kids' father who took every single opportunity to create havoc in my life. I was still hurting from my divorce from Gill. I was still mourning the loss of my sister, my brother, and my dad.

    I was still trying to figure out how to parent a daughter who is hurting deeply from a relationship with her dad that makes her feel unfulfilled and unloved. I am raising another son who has challenges making friends and is overly attached to me. I still saw myself as broken and unworthy. However, I began to feel the power of prayer. I began to feel like I wasn't pretending to pray anymore. I talked to Him like I would my best friend. I talked to Him about the things that I was struggling with before my feet hit the floor and did so not expecting Him to miraculously fix it for me, nor being angry that He didn't. I asked Him to help me recognize the things in my life that He put in my path to give me the strength that I was praying for so fervently.

Who Did You See?

Did I backtrack? Did I fail some or most days? Yes, but the difference is that I didn't shake my fist at Him because of all that "He" had let happen to me. I didn't beat myself up about it. I just laughed, no really, I laughed, and I said, okay, let's try that again. The more I laughed about my failure the more grace I not only gave myself, but I gave the people in my life -- past and present. The simple realization that I just had to quit caring "who people would see" began to bring me the peace that I had been looking for my entire life. For the very first time in my life I wasn't looking for a man to fill a place in my life. I wasn't looking for a distraction from my life. I wanted to be present for the moments that I had been letting pass me by. I found beauty in the stress, realizing that in some ways it had saved my life. I had not been ready to heal before now. I wish I had, but I had not. That isn't God's fault. That isn't my brother's fault. That isn't my mother's fault. That was my fault. I had been filling my life with situations, people, and distractions so that I never had to look back or even face the present. I chose those things, they weren't all chosen for me. I hurt myself because the pain felt familiar. I had to walk through every one of those single things to find myself and find how much God loved me through them.

I do not believe that God sits by and lets bad things happen to us. I do not believe that God chooses to not intervene. He gave us all free will. It is the greatest gift and the greatest curse to mankind. We all have complete control over what we do with it and I do believe that God hurt even more than I did during every single hurt and disappointment that I endured. God wanted better not only for me, but also for the people who hurt me. The hurt that they carry for the things they have done is keeping them from the peace, healing, and love that God wants for them. No amount of pain that I dreamed of inflicting on them for hurting me could hurt more than that separation from Him. There is peace in just wanting to be me, to be the best me I can be today.

Things Always Get Worse Before They Get Better

Do you think Satan would give up that easy? He had held me in a state of anger and disillusionment for a very long time so if you have gotten this far into the book, you know he didn't give up on me. My mother continued in her destructive behavioral patterns, just as I was struggling to hold onto the peace I was finding. There were days that I failed miserably, but I didn't beat myself up the way I had before. Then, at the gym on April 10, 2015, my trainer asked me to go to dinner with her and some friends. The kids were gone for the weekend. That is the night I met Alan Chastain, and had I not been spending all the time working on those wounds, I would not have been ready for what happened.

God had prepared this path, like every other path for me. Alan and I recognized in each other what had been missing in every other relationship we had. We both have been the glue for the people in our lives. We both had been the one who had to be strong when we felt weak. We both had been the one who ended up feeling like doing the right things had left us with the short end of the stick. We had trusted all the wrong people, for all the wrong reasons, and I immediately felt at peace with him. We sat on my back porch two days later and I felt like I was sitting there with my dad. He had the same way of looking at me, the same way he intently listened to my stories. He made me feel safe. I wasn't pretending with him. I wasn't showing him what I felt like he wanted to see. I was sitting on the porch without my mask, and he couldn't tear his eyes away from me.

I should have felt naked, I had never been truly vulnerable with a man before. We sat there all night telling our stories and I was absolutely falling in love with this man. We have not been apart since that night, well, other than his duty to the National Guard. We fell into step and we both knew that this was what we had been waiting for our whole lives. I cannot speak for Alan, but I do know that I would have never been ready for this before now. If God had put him in my path before I made the choice to start healing, I would have ruined it. Had I not gone through all the things I had, I wouldn't have chosen to begin the healing. So, if God had intervened, would I have gotten there?

As Alan and I fell into place, my mother continued to fall even deeper into depression and alcoholism. As I got healthier, she fell further into self-destruction which led to her decision to come into my room and tell me all those hurtful things. This was why I made her leave our house. God was in the background making me stronger. All the

Who Did You See?

days that I chose to want more led to a strength that I didn't know was there. I sit here today typing this story in the same bed, in the same room, in the same house where those hurtful words were spoken over me. I would have never had the strength to draw the line with her that I had to draw. I would have stood up and yelled back everything I had tucked away to hurt her back.

I would have told her all the horrible things that I thought about her all those years. I am much better at fighting than she is, and I held the power to destroy her at that moment, and I chose not to. I chose to close my eyes and pray when she started. I prayed for her and for me to choose to love her enough to just listen. God was with me then, being the parent I needed and she couldn't be—again. I know He sat here and His heart hurt as much as mine because He wanted her to have peace just as much as He wanted it for me. I know that God had been with me at all those other times in the dark when I was crying and hurting. God never left my side, I was just too angry to reach for his hand. I reached for it that day, and I found peace in a moment that I had been waiting for all those years. It wasn't my strength that kept me from falling apart, it was His. I didn't have to be strong enough to endure any of it, I just had had to lean into it holding His hand.

I began to let the anger toward her go that day. There have been days I have picked it back up but the burden of carrying it makes me want to put it back down. I am learning to recognize the signs of my own self-destruction like I recognize my mother's. I can't beat her up for doing the exact same things that I am doing, so I have found a way to give her the grace that she deserves. It isn't me being strong, it is me knowing that I am not expected to be strong enough to carry all the burden on my own.

She moved into an apartment with a roommate. My mom had always cared about how she was perceived (by everyone but me) and so I knew she would not let them see her drinking. She settled into a role there of caring for her roommate. Although she complained incessantly, I think it gave her purpose and we were both on our own journey. We were all healing quietly in our own way. Alan's son was settling in, which is another book in itself. The kids were adjusting to having a man in the house who wasn't chasing after their affection, which oddly made them feel completely at ease. We found happiness in our day-to-day life, which would have been the most boring existence to anyone else. The peace we have in our home together is immeasurable. We simply love each other. There is never a worry of how we will respond to the myriad of craziness that makes up our life.

With eight children, crazy ex-spouses, and life itself, our life is a constant battlefield. However, having each other makes it feel peaceful somehow.

Pamela Chastain

We Find Ourselves Back At the Beginning

So, we find ourselves back where I started this story to some extent. I found myself sick last year—sick to the point where I could not get out of bed most days. Surgeries ensued and I was literally stuck here in this same bed where I am typing. I had felt the need to journal for two years. It still scared me in that same irrational way that anything real scared me and made me run. I'm not gonna lie, I was high on some great pain medication so the battles both with myself and God about doing it was the stuff of a bad sitcom. I tried to increase my meds to make the voice quieter in my mind—it didn't work, but just made me constipated. I tried to watch trash television to get lost in other people's reality. Nope, none of it worked. So, I pulled out a spiral notebook and I wrote letters.

Years ago, Lindsay kept encouraging me to write letters to the people in my life. Every good therapist wants you to write the letters. I refused, I refused over and over again to put anything down on paper. That is what started this journey, those letters. I finally wrote them. I wrote a letter to my brother who abused me. I wrote a letter to my sister. I wrote a letter to my other brother. I wrote a letter to my dad, and I wrote a letter to little Pam.

Who Did You See?

Oddly, I didn't write a letter to my mom. I couldn't yet. I wrote them, and then I wrote the first chapter of this book.

My journey started there, simply testing myself more than anything. Could I crack open the door and not let the force of all of the things hiding behind that door knock me down? A million fears were wrapped up in opening that door, but I did it, and no one died. I didn't end up in the psychiatric ward. I didn't get in my car and go find and kill my brother. I didn't hit my mother over the head with her brandy bottle. I didn't punch the kids' father in the face. I didn't do anything but cry. I cried. I laughed. I lived through it.

Now that I had lived through it, what did this mean? Could I finish writing it? What would I do with it? I really was not sure. Just like every other time in my life, God showed up with his perfect timing. I saw a post from a friend from high school. He was starting his own publishing company and an author coaching program. He was looking for people who he could help write their story. I reached out to him and this journey began. Just like so many other times in my life, the path was there for me to walk it if I didn't run. God had once again offered healing in the form of someone who believed in me, someone who was there at just the right time and place when I needed them the most.

Pamela Chastain

God has been most represented in my life by the face of people who chose to love me when God laid it on their hearts. I hope that somehow I was a puzzle piece for their own life, as they were mine.

So, I began to write, I would like to tell you that I had this great plan. I would like to say I started making a plan about how to structure the book or what I thought should be the main purpose or something very logical like that. Nope, I started typing. In fact, typing this paragraph I haven't gone back and read it at all. I, once again, had a fear that if I went backward that I wouldn't keep moving forward. I wrote when I felt like I could, and I let this book come as I felt led to write. I needed time to process, and I also believe I needed the time in between to make sense of the healing that was coming from writing it. Instead of writing all the pain associated with the relationship with my mother, making me angrier with her and taking our relationship backward, it was giving me the strength to heal it. I am making peace with my mother, one day at a time. This book and the healing that God is doing in my heart is helping me to not only forgive her but love the many things that make her Johnnie Sue. I was so angry with her, I never found any beauty in who she was. I love my mom. She makes me crazy, but I love her anyway. In loving her, she is finding her own healing and taking off her own mask. It appears

Who Did You See?

that I got that honestly. I take such pride in all the traits I believe I got from my father and I have always denied any and all resemblance to my mother.

So here it goes. I look like my mother. I used to hide behind my mask like my mother. I was self-destructive like my mother. I also spent most of my life waiting for God to either save me from my circumstances or take me from my misery, like my mother. I blamed all the bad things that happened to me on my mother's choices to not protect me, like my mother. We are as alike as we are different and I am learning to be okay with that. I have often joked that if you questioned whether or not God had a sense of humor, just look at my life. I would go on to say that God had taken every person who loved me away and left me with the one person who had never chosen to love or protect me. That is how I have seen it my entire adult life. Having to write my story has changed my perspective on so many things. I still believe that God has a sense of humor—I just don't believe he laughs at my pain.

I know now that He was always there, always loving me, always whispering in my ear to be strong but not so strong that I wouldn't reach out for Him. To give up my anger for love. To love myself enough to be patient but keep moving forward toward the person I want to be. To love people where they are and not where I want them to be. He loved me enough to work all these things that people chose for my pain and hurt for my good. He loved me enough to put all these people in my life who would love me enough to plant seeds for only these good things to grow. He loved me enough to keep blessing me more than I could ever deserve with children who would love me without my mask. He loved me period, always and forever.

This journey isn't over, it is just beginning. I will fall, but I will get back up and reach out for His hand for the strength; not to survive but to be present in this amazing life He has given me. I want to end it with honesty, dignity, strength, and grace. I want to love, and be loved, for who I am and not who I believe you want me to be.

Who did you see? It doesn't matter to me now—that version is gone and a blur in a life that has taken me on so many roller coaster rides.

See me for who I am.

About the Author

Pamela Chastain is a native Tennessean, and other than a brief stint in Canada, has lived in the Nashville area her entire life. She is a proud wife to Alan, mother to Alec, Krista, and Jack, and grandmother to Abree. Pamela spent most of her career managing and consulting in the medical arena for more than twenty-five years. Her story is about her own sexual abuse and how her life was affected by the absence of support from the very family members who were supposed to shelter and protect her. Suffering immense loss, she began writing her story by writing letters to all the people who had been party to the abuse. Those "letters from her soul" ended up giving her the strength to write her own story. After hiding from the abuse for more than four decades, she found that opening up about the abuse helped to heal the scar. She wants to dedicate the rest of her life to sharing her story, and hopefully it can help others find their voices to tell their own stories.

Made in the USA
Columbia, SC
05 September 2020